CW01082503

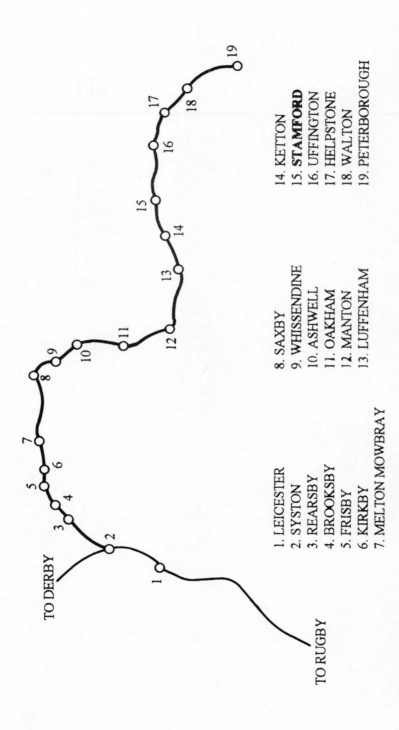

TO DERBY

TO RUGBY

1. LEICESTER
2. SYSTON
3. REARSBY
4. BROOKSBY
5. FRISBY
6. KIRKBY
7. MELTON MOWBRAY

8. SAXBY
9. WHISSENDINE
10. ASHWELL
11. OAKHAM
12. MANTON
13. LUFFENHAM

14. KETTON
15. **STAMFORD**
16. UFFINGTON
17. HELPSTONE
18. WALTON
19. PETERBOROUGH

MIDLAND RAILWAY (SYSTON & PETERBOROUGH RAILWAY) 1848

STAMFORD -ALL CHANGE!

How the Railway
Came to Stamford

ARTHUR & ELISABETH JORDAN

AMPHION PRESS

A Midland 2-2-2 passenger engine No 60 built by Sharp & Co. in 1848.
(Arthur Jordan Collection)

Front cover illustration

In 1952 Toton-based LMS Beyer-Garratt No 47997, fitted with rotating bunker,
hauls a down freight through Stamford.
The Seaton push-pull train stands in the bay platform. *(P.H. Wells)*

Title page illustration

The initials S.P.R. still show clearly in the weather vane
surmounting the bell-tower. *(Elisabeth Jordan)*

Published by Amphion Press, Station House, Stamford, Lincolnshire PE9 2JN

Printed in England by E & E Plumridge Ltd of Cambridge

Designed & Typeset by Tim Plumridge

ISBN No 0 9516563 1 7

INTRODUCTION

A passenger arriving at Stamford's temporary station in 1846 would have heard the porter call "ALL CHANGE! STAMFORD - ALL CHANGE!" This was an instruction to alight, since the line from Peterborough, at this time, went no further.

However, the railway was to result in considerable change, in Stamford; to its markets, industries and links with the rest of the country.

For this account of the coming of the railway to Stamford we have drawn heavily on the files of the Stamford Mercury, to the Editor of which we are extremely grateful. We make no apology for quoting extensively verbatim as we believe that the style of reporting and amount of lineage devoted to railway news indicate the importance attached to the rail connection.

We are also appreciative of the assistance given by the House of Lords' Record Office; Record Offices at Northampton, Lincoln and Derby; Libraries at Stamford, Northampton and Lincoln; and Stamford Museum. The plans are by Paul Harkin.

This account is concerned primarily with the Midland Railway's Syston & Peterborough line reaching Stamford in 1846 and 1848 although brief reference is made to developments up to 1853.

All fares and charges are expressed in pre-decimal coinage; i.e. shillings as s. and pence as d. We can see no point in attempting to express these sums in the decimal currency since this would take no account of changes in prices, wages, rents etc.

The following abbreviations have been used for references in the text.

SM Stamford Mercury

NM Northampton Mercury

LC Lincolnshire Chronicle

CONTENTS

BEFORE THE RAILWAY

When the first inter-city railway in the world opened between Liverpool and Manchester in September 1830 land carriage elsewhere depended upon the horse. The so-called 'Golden Age of Coaching', begun around 1780, was at its peak. Most main roads had been improved under the various Turnpike Trusts and relays of fresh horses at coaching inns made possible speeds of as high as ten miles per hour. Coaches displayed evocative names such as 'The Comet' and 'The Flying Machine'.

Perhaps the busiest coaching route was the Great North Road connecting London to York and further north into Scotland. On this route Stamford was a kind of Crewe Junction with the clatter of horses hooves and the rumble of carriage wheels sounding throughout the twenty-four hours. Not only north-south coaches but east-west services made connections here.

Stamford was also connected to the inland and coastal waterway system by the Stamford Canal which ran parallel to the River Welland as far as Market Deeping and then joined that river to reach the Wash.

When the Liverpool & Manchester Railway Company obtained its Act of Parliament in 1826 there were already railways proposed that would link London directly with York. The 'Grand Northern' would run via Cambridge, Lincoln, Gainsborough and Selby, whilst a London & York scheme was also proposed by the Northern & Eastern Railway. It was one of these schemes which alarmed John Clare when, on June 4th, 1825, he recorded in his diary, 'Saw three fellows in Royce wood (near Clare's home in Helpston) who I found were laying out the plan for an "Iron Railway" from Manchester to London… I little thought that fresh intrusions would interrupt my solitudes after the Enclosure … they will despoil a boggy place that is famous for Orchises …"

Twenty years were to elapse before a railway came near Clare's 'boggy place'. In the meantime London became linked to the Liverpool & Manchester Railway by the Grand Junction Railway (1837) and the London & Birmingham Railway (1838). The L&BR avoided the county town of Northampton, intending a station at Blisworth, four miles distant, to serve as a railhead for the surrounding district.

However, the railway made an impact on Stamford even at a distance of 40 miles, for when the line opened between London and the 'Denbigh Hall' inn (a temporary station near Wolverton) in April 1838 a number of coaches abandoned the road between Stamford and London, instead making for the 'Denbigh Hall' to connect with the new railway.

A NEW RAILWAY COACH called THE GREYHOUND
from Grantham to London.
Grantham to Denbigh Hall Tues., Thurs. & Sats. 7am via
Stamford, Oundle, Thrapston, Wellingborough, Olney, Newport
Pagnell arriving Denbigh Hall for the 5pm train.
Leaves Denbigh Hall every Mon. Weds. & Fri. after first train from London.

The missing link in the London & Birmingham line between the 'Denbigh Hall' and Rugby was completed and the line opened throughout in September 1838 whereupon coaches from Stamford and beyond now made the rail connection at Blisworth.

In 1844 three railway companies were amalgamated to form the Midland Railway which made a connection with the L&BR at Rugby and ran through Leicester and Derby to Leeds, with a branch to Nottingham and a connection with the York & North Midland at Normanton, thus providing a through rail route from London to York. This was, to say the least, a circuitous route and not surprisingly the proposal for a London & York direct railway was revived.

The prospect of loss of traffic to such a rival prompted the L&BR and the MR to prepare opposition to this London & York direct line both inside and outside Parliament. One tactic was to throw out tentacles from their existing systems eastwards into the territory through which the London & York intended to pass.

For the L&BR this took the form of a 'Blisworth & Peterborough Branch' passing through Northampton, Wellingborough, Thrapston, Oundle and Wansford (Sibson) to make an end-on connection with an Eastern Counties Railway line from London via Cambridge, Ely, and March. Opened in June 1845, Wansford (Sibson) station, on the Great North Road, became the coach/rail interchange for Stamford and a wide area to the north.

The speedier travel by rail was immediately apparent in Stamford:
Going to London, transacting business there, and returning home a hundred miles on the same day, has often been referred to as the "ne plus ultra" of accommodation in travelling. The point is now attained. A lady residing at Stamford went to town on Saturday last by the 7 o'clock train in the morning, [i.e. from Wansford] spent four hours there and engaged a governess, and returned to her home by the evening train, with much less fatigue than lately attended the day's travelling by coach up to London only.
(NM 13 June 1845)

Special single-fare tickets for the return journey were made available in connection with Stamford races from Northampton, Wellingborough, Oundle and Peterborough. Coach operators quickly adjusted their routes to feed into the new railways as they opened.

GENERAL COACH AND RAILWAY OFFICE.

George Hotel, Stamford.

H. Whincup respectfully announces to the public that on and after 2d. of June next coaches and omnibuses will leave the hotel in time for the undermentioned trains.

LONDON & BIRMINGHAM RAILWAY

To the Wansford and Sibson station (up trains)

Leave	Arrive	Arrive
Stamford 6am	London 12am	Birmingham 11am
	Manchester 2.30pm	Liverpool 3.30pm
Stamford 9.45am	London 3.30pm	Birmingham 3.30pm
	Manchester 7pm	Liverpool 8pm
Stamford 3.15pm	London 8.30	Birmingham 10pm
Stamford - mail	London 5pm	
train 12 night		

From the Wansford and Sibson station (down trains)

Leave	Arrive	Arrive
London 6am	Sibson 10.45	Stamford 11.45
London 10.30am	Sibson 2.30	Stamford 3.30
London 4pm	Sibson 8.20	Stamford 9.20
London		
mail train 9pm	Sibson 12.55	Stamford 1.55

The Lincoln Tally Ho coach will leave the Saracen's Head, Lincoln, every morning (Sundays excepted) at half past 9 o'clock, arrive at Sleaford half past 11, Falkingham half past 12, Bourn at half past 1, Stamford quarter before 3, and London at half past 8. Will leave London at half past 10, arrive at Stamford half past 3 and at Lincoln by 9 the same evening travelling the whole distance in about 10 and a half hours.

Fares as under:

			Inside	Outside
Lincoln	to	Sleaford	7s	4s
Lincoln	to	Falkingham	10s	6s
Lincoln	to	Bourn	13s	8s
Lincoln	to	Greatford	14s	9s
Lincoln	to	Stamford	16s	10s
Lincoln	to	London	£1 15s	£1 3s
London	to	Stamford	£1	14s
London	to	Greatford	£1 2s	15s
London	to	Bourn	£1 5s	17s
London	to	Falkingham	£1 7s	18s 6d
London	to	Sleaford	£1 10s 6d	£1
London	to	Lincoln	£ 15s	£1 3s

The Wonder will leave the George Hotel, Grantham, every morning (Sundays excepted) at half past 7, arrive at the Bull Inn, Witham Common, at 35 minutes past 8, Stamford 45 minutes past 9, London half past 3. Will leave London at half past 10am, and arrive at Grantham at half past 5pm.

Fares

Grantham	to	Stamford	9s	5s
Grantham	to	London	£1 9s	19s
London	to	Stamford	£1	14s
London	to	Grantham	£1 9s	19s

Omnibus fares

Stamford to and from Sibson station inside 2s, outside 1s 6d. Coaches will also start from the George Hotel, Stamford, to Cambridge, Nottingham, Leicester, and other places as usual. Post horses, chaises, flys, etc may always be had at the George Hotel, Stamford, and at the Sibson station at reasonable prices.

H. W. has also entered into an engagement with Messrs Chaplin and Horne, to convey goods and merchandise of almost every description at very moderate charges, the particulars of which will appear in a future advertisement on the commencement of the carrying of such goods.

George Hotel, St Martins, Stamford 28th May 1845 (SM 30 May 1845)

As a coaching inn the main entrance of the George Hotel faced the Great North Road, i.e. High Street St. Martin's. With the opening of the railway a main entrance was made in Station Road. This, in turn, has been blocked up and most guests arriving by car now enter the hotel from the hotel car park. *(Elisabeth Jordan)*

As the railway advanced nearer to Stamford so coach operators adjusted their routes to make rail connections, as in the case of the Stamford & Peterborough line reaching Melton Mowbray in September 1846. It was advertised that the 'Railway Times' would in future leave the George, Stamford ' ... at 10 minutes before 8 o'clock... and arrive at Melton in time for the 10.30 train which reaches Syston at 11 o'clock, Derby and Nottingham at 12, Leeds 3.30, Sheffield 1.40 and all parts of the north.'

During the so-called 'Golden Age of Coaching' the turnpike trusts along the Great North Road, and those controlling roads feeding into it, had enjoyed prosperity but, already by 1848, they were experiencing a falling-off in traffic and so in revenue.

At a meeting held at The George & Angel, Stamford, the trustees of roads leading out of Stamford found no bidders for the Horn Lane toll bar (on the Great North Road near Exton Park), even after offering a reduction of £84 on the previous year's £484. It was decided to appoint their own toll collector for a year to ascertain the real value of the tolls.

Stamford toll bar, once let for £1,760 and offered at the 1847 rental of £667, was finally let for only £454, a reduction of £213. Ryhall bar reduced from £423 to £325; the Bull bar reduced from £211 to £56. 'The reason assigned for so large a decrease is the introduction of railways in the neighbourhood'.(SM 14 January 1848).

However, the opening of a railway could result in a considerable increase in the volume of road traffic to and from a station, as at Luffenham after the opening of the Syston & Peterborough line in June 1848. In October of that year the trustees for the turnpike between Morcott and Luffenham were considering erecting an additional toll bar 'to protect the interests of the road'. The Great Northern's station at Tallington, opened in 1852, generated additional road traffic to and from Stamford so that the Deeping & Morcott Turnpike Trustees were able to increase the rental of the Newstead bar from £475 to £600 per annum in 1853.

From the opening of the Liverpool & Manchester Railway in 1830 the Post Office realised the advantages of rail over road for the speedy transport of mail switching the Liverpool - London mail to rail as far as Newton. The London & Birmingham Railway's Blisworth & Peterborough branch (often referred to as the Northampton & Peterborough Railway) resulted in significant changes in Stamford's postal arrangements allowing a midnight departure from Stamford with London mail via Wansford station, whilst mail from London arrived in Stamford at 1.55am, an improvement of several hours. Not surprisingly, there was now talk of a rail link between Stamford and Wansford, but more of this later.

The Lincoln mail coach had its route altered to run via Stamford instead of Peterborough, that city receiving its mail from London direct by the London & Birmingham Railway. Mail for Louth, Grimsby and Barton-on-Humber was loaded in a horse-drawn mail coach at the General Post Office, London. Taken to Euston station, the coach was loaded onto a flat rail truck and conveyed to Peterborough where horses waited to haul it by road to Louth.

Midland Railway tentacles into likely London & York direct territory were a line from Nottingham to Lincoln and another, the subject of this book, from Syston, north of Leicester, through Melton Mowbray, Oakham and Stamford to Peterborough, promoted by the Midland Railway as the 'Syston & Peterborough Railway'. From its promotion through to its completion this line encountered many difficulties, not least problems with two noble lords, the Earl of Harborough and the Marquess of Exeter.

The Royal Mail coach for Louth being loaded onto the Peterborough train at Euston.

(Arthur Jordan Collection)

THE SYSTON & PETERBOROUGH LINE

The construction of any new railway impinged upon the rights of others. Land had to be acquired, usually under powers of compulsory purchase. It was often necessary to reroute highways, stop-up streets in towns, and give the railway the right of precedence at level-crossings. Bridges had to be built and buildings tunnelled under, whilst rivers, canals and drainage channels might need to be diverted. Further, the new company required extensive powers to raise large sums of capital, to regulate the conduct of users of the railway, and to make connections with the lines of other companies. These were powers far beyond those available to private individuals and the only means of obtaining them was through a private Act of Parliament.

For this purpose the first stage was to present a Bill to the House of Commons supported by plans and elevations defining the proposed line and evidence that the required capital would be raised. Then the House would set up a Select Committee comprising interested Members before which would appear witnesses to give evidence in support of the proposals, and others in opposition to those proposals.

If and when the Bill passed the Commons it went to the House of Lords where the whole procedure would be repeated, and only if passed by both Houses would it become an Act and construction be allowed to proceed.

The Midland Railway obtained 'An Act to empower the Midland Railway Company to make a branch from the said Railway near Syston in the County of Leicester to the City of Peterborough (30th June 1845)' From then on this line is referred to as the 'Syston & Peterborough Railway' which may cause some confusion but it never was a separate company. Authorisation was given to raise the sum of £750,000 by new shares or stock.

As proposed, the course of the Syston & Peterborough line (48 miles) was to leave the existing Midland Railway line at Syston, about five miles north of Leicester, and head north-eastwards along the valley of the River Wreake to Melton Mowbray.

This drawing of Peterborough Eastern Counties station, opened in 1845, illustrates the Tudor style adopted by J.W. Livock. *(Illustrated London News)*

From here it would take an easterly course to Saxby and there turn southwards to pass through Oakham to Manton, where a turn eastwards following the valleys of the Rivers Chater and Welland would take it to Stamford and on through Uffington to Helpston. Here a turn south-eastwards would bring the line to Peterborough where a junction with the London & Birmingham was made.

The Northampton & Peterborough branch of the London & Birmingham Railway (London & North Western from 1846) reached Peterborough in 1845, intending to connect with the Eastern Counties, although the latter's line from Shoreditch, London via

STAMFORD – ALL CHANGE

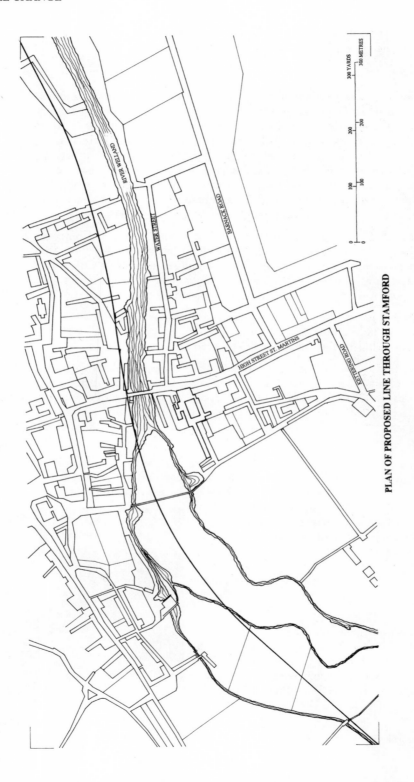

PLAN OF PROPOSED LINE THROUGH STAMFORD

RIVER WELLAND

WATER STREET

BARNACK ROAD

HIGH STREET ST. MARTINS

KETTERING ROAD

0   100   200   300 YARDS
0   100   200   300 METRES

This scene would have looked very different had the line been built as originally proposed. Approaching from the west it would have passed through the Meadows. crossing the river here, into Bath Row then by a level crossing at the foot of St Mary's Hill. *(Robert Humm)*

Cambridge, Ely and March, did not reach Peterborough until 1847. However, the Eastern Counties constructed their station (later known as East) in time for use by both the LNW and the Syston & Peterborough branch of the Midland Railway.

Plans for the proposed Syston & Peterborough line, deposited with the House of Commons, showed it approaching Stamford from the west by crossing the Welland where the King's mill stream branches off, next through what was then known as Bull meadow, across the footpath from Wothorpe Road to Castle Dyke, over the river again to Bath Row, within a few yards of the town bridge. Here, houses occupied by Messrs George, Bunning, Pinney and Ayres would be demolished.

It would cross the Great North Road at the foot of St Mary's Hill on the level to pass along Wharf Road, which would be stopped-up. In the area between Wharf Road and St Mary's Place a station would be located. The Act required the Company:

> … to make a sufficient Bridge for Foot Passengers across the said Railway at the place where the same crosses the said Road number 22 [Great North Road] and the said Railway shall not be opened for traffic until such Footbridge shall have been completed.

A further precaution against accidents, having regard to the volume of road traffic crossing the town bridge, was stipulated in the Act:

> … that all trains on the said Railway shall be made to stop before arriving at such Road, and shall not cross the same at any greater Speed than Four Miles an Hour.

Riverside warehouses near the bridge would be demolished and other properties, including The Boat Inn, along the line as far as Earl Brownlow's gardens. (A list of properties affected is given in the Appendix). Crossing the river at a point south of St Leonard's Priory, the line would run south of Hudd's Mill to cross the river again near its confluence with the Gwash.

The proposed crossing at the foot of St Mary's Hill was to be one cause of opposition to the Bill, another being at Saxby, where the line would cross Stapleford Park, seat of Lord Harborough, who also had an interest in the Oakham Canal which would be adversely affected by the railway. The proprietor of the Nene Navigation petitioned against the Bill claiming that the railway would destroy river traffic. However, it was revealed that he had already sold land to another railway company. The supporters of a London & York Railway also opposed the line.

The Marquess of Exeter signed a petition presented to the House of Commons opposing the railway crossing the main road at the foot of St Mary's Hill but there was popular support among Stamford people for the line following this course, as the Stamford Mercury reported:

On Wednesday evening Sir George Clerk presented to the House of Commons a petition signed by the Marquess of Exeter, and by a few persons in Stamford whom he influences to any extent, complaining that the line of the Syston & Peterborol railway is set to cross at the foot of the bridge in Stamford on a level with the turnpike. Not a word is said of the bridge itself, which is the narrowest and most dangerous nuisance between London and Edinburgh, and at which bridge Lord Exeter receives a toll for repairing it for the public convenience. The opinion of the town at large on this precious petition was conclusively shown at a meeting of the Town Council on Tuesday. The Mayor (Chas. Haycock Esq.) had, to the surprise of all persons conversant with municipal matters, introduced into the notice paper a passage in which one of the councillors, Mr. Rd. Thompson, described as the most arrogant and improper in its style and purpose that he had ever witnessed. It was in these words 'To sanction a petition to the House of Commons objecting to that part of the intended "Syston & Peterboro' railway" which crosses on a level with the street at the north end of the town bridge within the said borough, and to order the corporate seal to be affixed thereto.' Mr. Thompson remarked that, to enter upon the discussion to which such notice would give rise, could not fail to occasion indignant expressions and bitter division in the Council: a slight rumour, even, of the notice, had already produced the greatest excitement amongst the inhabitants in general of the Borough. He, therefore, for the love of peace and good fellowship, which would be so greatly damaged by entering upon the subject, moved that it be entirely passed over by the Council. After a few observations by other members, Mr. Thompson's judgement in this matter was fully sustained in a division, which gave a minority of five councillors for entering upon the discussion of the Mayor's proposition and a majority of thirteen for passing it over without any further notice. Thus this bold and most irregular course of seeking to attach the corporate seal to a petition prepared out of the hall by Lord Exeter's agents, and brought up for furthering the noble Lord's desperate opposition to a public measure for which nine-tenths of the householders of Stamford, and numerous respectable individuals of the neighbourhood, have repeatedly, at public meetings and by petitions, expressed the strongest desire, has eminently recoiled upon the projectors and the abetters of so covert and unworthy a proceeding. So strongly was the injustice and indignity of the course taken by Lord Exeter's adherents felt in the town that, as soon as it transpired on Monday evening, memorials to the council were immediately prepared from each of the six parishes and were signed in two hours the next morning by more than 630 burgesses, cautioning the members 'not to listen to the suggestion of persons who are unfriendly to the measure of a railway at all, and requesting that the Council will not sanction any proposition calculated in any degree whatever to impede the passing of the Bill for the Syston & Peterboro' railway.' Respectable inhabitants of each parish attended at the Town Hall with these memorials but, in consequence of the turn which the business took in the Council room, it was deemed better that they should not be admitted, and on being informed of the resolution of the members by a large majority not to lend themselves to the Mayor's views, as shown by his extraordinary notice, they departed well satisfied with the signal victory which their principles had obtained.   (SM 21 March 1845)

A petition in support of the railway as proposed and signed by 2,168 persons, which included nearly the whole adult male population of Stamford as well as many gentry and farmers of the district, was presented to Parliament in April 1845 when the Bill received its second reading without opposition. It would be in Committee that opposition would be voiced:

> Lord Exeter's endeavour to harm it will be made in the committee and for that purpose several of his tenants and retainers have been required to hold themselves in readiness to go to London within a few days to give evidence against it: one or two are to allege an absence of notice of intended appropriation of sites by the railway company, but the larger number are to speak to the amount of traffic over the bridge and to bolster up the bugbear of danger from crossing the road at the north end of that precious piece of pontage. The sudden tenderness of the Marquess of Exeter for the people of Stamford as respects this locality of the bridge is one of the finest pieces of humbug that the future historian of the Borough will have to record. It has been for ages a crying nuisance … The engineer and directors of the railway have pledged themselves to build a new safe and commodious bridge instead of this pet breakneck of the Marquess of Exeter, which he holds in terrorem, over the lieges of the town: but, ah! he will not have it so: the bad bridge serves the turn of preventing persons from being attracted to the town and therein he finds his account, and keeps the bridle in the mouth of those who are born to live only by his permission.   (SM 4 April 1845)

The possibility of a railway crossing at the foot of St. Mary's Hill and right on the end of the bridge in 1845 alarmed some Stamford people. In 1996 road vehicles cause equal concern.
(Elisabeth Jordan)

Before the Parliamentary Committee a number of Stamford inhabitants, suspected of 'being confederated for the purpose of defeating the Bill', directed their opposition to the siting of the proposed station and the direction the line was to take through the town.

Stamford's medieval town bridge, over which passed the traffic of the Great North road, had a carriageway of only eight feet, with refuges over the cutwaters for pedestrians. Only wide enough for the passage of one vehicle, the result was considerable congestion and frequent contretemps.

Here is an example of the congestion which could occur on the bridge:

> From the narrowness of Stamford bridge between 60 and 70 stoppages were experienced during

Thursday the 10th inst. (the day of the new Spring Fair). A few days previously some amusement was afforded to many onlookers. A clergyman residing in the neighbourhood was proceeding in his phaeton towards St Martin's and a man in a cart was coming into the town: both vehicles were on the bridge at the same time, and as each driver contended that he was on the narrow passage first, neither would 'back'. The parson stared at the rustic, and the latter at the former, whilst the horses rubbed their noses together. Silence was at last broken and an altercation continued for a long time, but the clergyman not showing the superiority of his feelings as a gentleman and a disciple of humility, the other set the example of giving way and room was made for 'His Reverence' to pass. (SM 18 April 1845)

It was understandably envisaged that a railway crossing on the north end of the bridge, with a station nearby, would add further to this congestion. A census of bridge traffic for one week was presented to the Select Committee in support of a proposal, thought to have emanated from the Marquess, for the station to be located on the south side of the bridge:

Fred Burton, clerk to Mr. Jeremiah Clapton of Stamford, proved that he was engaged for two weeks to take an account of the traffic across Stamford bridge. The first week's return from March 24 to March 29, the time being from 7 o'clock in the morning to 7 in the evening, was as follows: foot passengers, 25,730; two-horse carriages, 116; one-horse carriages, 776; men on horseback, 612; passengers in carriages, 1,690; carts and waggons, 560; horses in waggons, 914; horses, 216; oxen, 52; sheep, 1,687. The foot passengers that passed on the Tuesday were 3,485, and on Friday, the market day, 6,782. On a Fair day, April 10th, the foot passengers were 7,747; sheep, 4,282; oxen, 401.

(SM 2 May 1845)

From these figures it is not possible to disentangle the four-horsed stage and mail coaches.

Whilst George Stephenson gave evidence supporting the course of the line as proposed in the Bill, another eminent engineer, Francis Giles, argued that a station at the back of the town was preferable to the one proposed. His Lordship had engaged Giles to survey a line which would have placed the station on the north side of the town. Giles confirmed that this was the Marquess's suggestion. In his evidence to the Select Committee of the House of Commons, Giles said: 'I would leave it [the proposed S&PR line] on the south side of Oakham and come by way of Empingham to the north side of Stamford, and not cross the river until below Stamford.'

In the 1840s Broad Street was the northernmost street of the town, running a few yards inside the line of the demolished medieval town wall, later followed by North Street. Beyond Broad Street lay open fields, common fields, many hovels, alehouses and brothels. This land belonged to the Burghley Estate and the Marquess, for whatever reasons, was prepared to have a station on it.

On being closely questioned before the Committee, Francis Giles conceded that trains would approach the station from the west down an incline of 1:106, but that he would arrange for a level stretch of 1,000 feet through the station. He considered that a station in this position would be much more convenient for the whole town and give easy access to the fairs and markets.

Among leading figures in favour of the Broad Street station were Sir George Clerk, a candidate in the 1847 election; Joseph Phillips, brewer and ex-Mayor of Stamford, and Joseph Cook Grant, owner of the foundry and farm machinery works. To say, as one historian does, that 'The Marquess resisted the proposal to run the line along the north bank of the river through land owned by Earl Brownlow. Instead he fought for a route along the south side which ran through his own land', does not tell the whole story.

The owner of the Stamford Mercury, a political opponent of the Marquess, took another opportunity to loose a few barbs at His Lordship:

> The third reading of the Syston Railway Bill was to have been moved in the House of Commons on Tuesday afternoon by Sir John Trollope Bart., but after the very favourable report of the committee on the Bill had been brought up the Marquess of Granby, we understand, proposed an amendment respecting the passing of the railway on the level of the road at Stamford bridge, and it was agreed to refer to the Select Committee on the Standing Orders an inquiry where the part of the Bill should be struck out (so, we believe, that the line may for a year stop on the west side of the bridge). Thus the matter rests at present, but we have the pleasure of saying that Mr. Hudson [Chairman of the Midland Railway] and the other officials connected with the measure, are as sanguine as ever that the Bill will pass triumphantly through both Houses of Parliament, sustained as it is by very favourable reports from both the Board of Trade and the Committee of the House of Commons, and immense as the benefit of the railway will be to a large district of the country through which it will pass. The Marquess of Exeter lately offered to forego his opposition to it on the payment of £40,000 by the Midland Company for certain property which he offered to them. Of the offer of certain other property in the town to his Lordship by the Corporation, at a price that is deemed by many persons monstrously under the market value, the noble Marquess observed 'I think the valuation extremely high'. The contrast between his views in the two cases is an amusing subject of conversation in Stamford. However, we can take it that, high as Lord Exeter's estimate of his own property is, the Midland Company have actually offered him £30,000 for it, in order if possible to reconcile him to the great improvement of the town which the railway would occasion ... (SM 23 May 1845)

ANNO OCTAVO & NONO

VICTORIÆ REGINÆ.

Cap. lvi.

An Act to empower the *Midland* Railway Company to make a Branch from the said Railway near *Syston* in the County of *Leicester* to the City of *Peterborough.* [30th *June* 1845.]

WHEREAS by virtue of several Acts of Parliament Railways have been made from *Rugby* viâ *Leicester* to *Nottingham* and *Derby,* by a Company called " The *Midland Counties* Railway Company," and from *Birmingham* to *Derby* by a Company called " The *Birmingham and Derby Junction* Railway Company," and from *Derby* to *Leeds* by a Company called " The *North Midland* Railway Company :" And whereas an Act was passed in the last Session of Parliament, intituled *An Act to consolidate the* 7 & 8 Vict. North Midland, Midland Counties, *and* Birmingham and Derby c. 18. Junction *Railways,* whereby the said Companies were united into One, under the Name of " The *Midland* Railway Company," and the said Railways, and all Branches thereof respectively, were vested in the said united Company, under the Name of the *Midland* Railways: And whereas it would be attended with great local and public Advantage if a Branch Railway were made from the said *Midland* [*Local.*] 14 O Railways

News of the passing of the Act authorising the construction of the Syston & Peterborough branch of the Midland Railway was greeted in Stamford by the ringing of bells throughout the day.

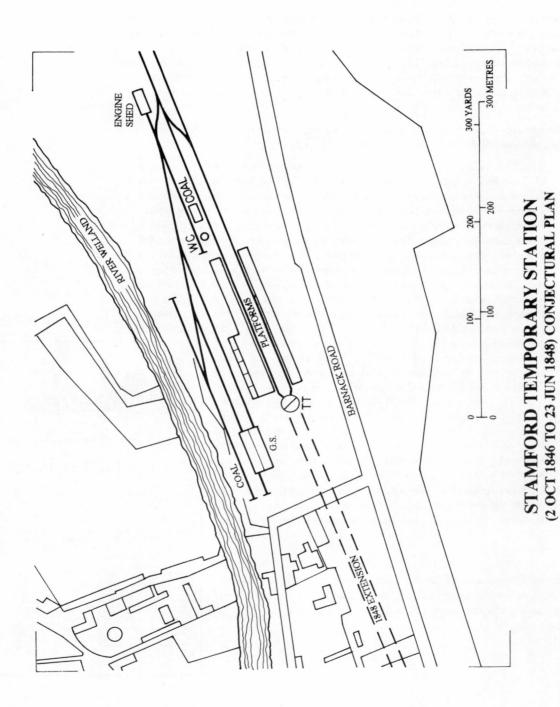

STAMFORD TEMPORARY STATION
(2 OCT 1846 TO 23 JUN 1848) CONJECTURAL PLAN

TRAINS AT LAST

In September 1845 this notice appeared in local newspapers:

MIDLAND RAILWAY
SYSTON & PETERBOROUGH RAILWAY
CONTRACT FOR WORKS

The Directors of the Midland Railway will meet at the railway station, Derby, on Tuesday the 7th of October, to receive tenders for the execution of the following works on the Syston & Peterboro' Railway.

Part 1. From Syston to Melton, being a distance of 91 miles, or thereabouts.

Part 2. From Peterboro' to Stamford, being a distance of 12 miles or thereabouts.

Plans, sections, drawings and specifications will be ready for inspection at the railway station, Leicester, on Tuesday the 16th instant, on which day the engineer will attend at 10 o'clock to make arrangements as to the measurement of the works with parties who may be proposing to tender and are then present. The Directors do NOT bind themselves to accept the lowest tender. All tenders must be delivered to the secretary at the railway station, Derby, before 10 o'clock am on Tuesday the 7th of October when all parties tendering are requested to be in attendance.

George Hudson, Chairman of the Board of Directors
John Ellis, Deputy Chairman
J. F. Bell, Secretary
By Order, Derby September 9 1845
(SM 12 September 1845)

Engineer for this line was Charles Liddell. It will be noted that tenders were not yet invited for the Melton to Stamford section. The decision for a deviation of the line at Stamford to take it along the south side of the river by a tunnel under St Martin's High Street, with a station in the George close, meant that there would be considerable delay before the line could be completed throughout. It was therefore intended to open the section between Peterborough and Stamford without delay in order to commence revenue earning operations. For this a temporary station of wooden construction would be sited at the end of Water Street behind the Union House. For the twelve miles between Peterborough and Stamford the seven contractors submitting tenders were told that the work should be completed by June 1846.

Such was the profitability of most early railways that speculators were tempted to invest in almost any scheme irrespective of its likely viability. So there began a 'Railway Mania' when the Stamford Mercury, along with all newspapers, carried a four page supplement containing 18 columns of railway notices in November 1845. Several schemes for other railways to serve Stamford were proposed and will be explained in a later chapter.

The Midland Railway had several costly schemes in hand at the same time as the Syston & Peterborough line, consequently there were occasions when financial considerations affected the commencement of the works. This explains why the company decided to concentrate work on the Syston to Melton Mowbray and Peterborough to Stamford sections, both of which, it was anticipated, would provide revenue because of their connection with existing lines. There were also the still unresolved difficulties with Lord Harborough at Saxby.

In December 1845 it was reported that the few men employed at Bainton had been laid off and that no further progress would be made during the winter. Nothing had been done at Stamford other than setting out the line. However, a week later, about a hundred men were said to be at work between Bainton and Maxey. In January 1846 men were engaged on constructing the line near the Crescent in Peterborough and work near the Union House at Stamford (site of the temporary station) had commenced in March 1846.

Heavy rains in April 1846 caused serious flooding east of Stamford when water reached within six inches of the top of the trackbed formation causing the movement of contractor's trains to be suspended. The following month the prospects of an early completion to Stamford seemed likely:

> The works between Stamford and Peterboro' are progressing rapidly, and there is now reason to believe the single line of rails will be open for the accommodation of passengers by the time originally mentioned, viz. the 1st of July. From Peterboro' to Bainton the works are nearly completed, the rails being in several places permanently laid for a double line. In the neighbourhood of Helpstone also the works are in a state of forwardness and to hasten the completion a locomotive was yesterday placed on the rails for the conveyance of materials to those parts where the road is not yet of the requisite elevation. In Pilsgate meadows several gangs of workmen are engaged filling up the hollows, but in this part the progress is necessarily retarded owing to the distance from which the soil and gravel for the foundations have to be obtained. It is expected however, that in the course of three weeks, the works will be sufficiently advanced to admit of the laying down of rails from Uffington bridge to the meadows opposite Hudd's Mills where an engine will be put on to traverse backwards and forwards with materials. The permanent rails are laid for rather more than a mile east of the Stamford Union house, but they will be shifted a little from their position as soon as the road is made broad enough for a double line. At the cutting by the Union, and in the close where the temporary station is to be erected, the men work night and day, a gang of about 20 relieving a gang of the same number at nightfall. It is understood that the temporary station will be a wooden building, and that as little expense as possible will be incurred in its erection as immediately after the passing (in the House of Lords) of the Bill for the deviations and branches, contracts will be received for the grand station in the George close. It is believed that within two months after the opening of the line from Peterboro' to Stamford a double line of rails will have been completed for the whole distance. (SM 15 May 1846)

At the east end of Stamford tunnel where the temporary station was located. The line terminated before the commencement of the curve. A turntable was positioned here both to turn the engines and to switch them from the up to the down line.
(Elisabeth Jordan)

Here it must be explained that the London & Birmingham's line from Blisworth and Northampton intended to use the Eastern Counties' station at Peterborough. When the L&B line opened in June 1845 the Eastern Counties line had not reached that city, and did not do so until January 1847, but it constructed its Peterborough station in time for use by L&B trains.

The Syston & Peterborough line was also to use that station, which was reached over the L&B (by 1846 the London & North Western Railway) by a junction 400 yards west of the station. This explains why, when the Peterborough to Stamford section of the Midland Railway was ready for inspection by Captain Coddington of the Board of Trade, early in 1846, a Midland engine and two carriages had to reach Stamford from Rugby via Blisworth and Peterborough. In August Stamford's temporary station was nearing completion:

> The exterior of the temporary station at Stamford for the Syston & Peterboro' railway is completed, and workmen are now busily engaged in levelling the ground for the safe approach of vehicles. About 100 yards from the office a spacious turntable is in the course of construction, the object of which has puzzled many visitors to the work. In the midst of a large stone-paved basin a strong stem or dwarf pillar has been built in which the spindle of the table will be inserted; and when finished it will be used for changing the engines from the up to the down line. The day for opening the railway has not yet been fixed. (SM 21 August 1846)

In addition to the facilities described above, an engine shed and goods warehouse were nearing completion, although only of a temporary construction as they would be moved elsewhere when Stamford's permanent station opened. A report in the Lincolnshire Chronicle & Northampton, Rutland & Nottingham Advertiser stated that: '…the platform for the arrival train is not yet completed'.

At the Peterborough end the station, which for a year had accommodated the

London & Birmingham trains, was being extended to cope with both the Midland and Eastern Counties traffic:

> Three breadths of roofing extending over a space of 411 feet by 127 connect the platform and shelter the numerous engines and carriages which now appear to be continually traversing the large field of rails called the terminus; a refreshment room and waiting rooms with several sleeping apartments are in process of erection; and numerous buildings are talked of as likely to be required for the companies about to jostle each other at Peterborough. (SM 4 Sep 1846)

So, the Midland Railway having no physical connection with the Syston & Peterborough line, arrangements were made for it to be worked by the Eastern Counties Railway, another of the Midland Chairman, George Hudson's lines, but this could not take place until that company's line from Ely to Peterborough had been opened which would not be until January of the following year. Consequently, from October 1846 until January 1847, trains were worked by the London & North Western Railway between Peterborough and Stamford. Stations at Walton, Helpstone, Uffington and Stamford were also staffed by the LNW.

With Peterborough Fair taking place on Friday and Saturday, October 2nd and 3rd, the company was anxious to have the line opened to carry the anticipated crowds, therefore it was fortuitous that Captain Coddington, Inspector of Railways, certified the line as being in a proper state for traffic on the evening of Thursday October 1st.

There was no impressive opening, the first public announcement that trains would run to Peterborough was by Stamford's town crier at half-past seven on Friday morning:

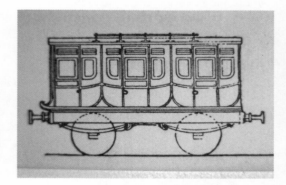

A Midland 2-2-2 passenger engine No 26 built by E.B. Wilson in 1847.

A Midland Railway First Class coupe carriage of 1848. Stagecoach influence in design is obvious. Luggage was carried on the roof.

(Arthur Jordan collection)

… there was a respectable number of passengers by the first three or four trains, and there would undoubtedly have been many more had it not been for unfavourable weather. On Saturday, it being very fine, nearly every train was filled, and the number of spectators was immense. The return trains in the middle of the day were comparatively empty, but towards evening they began to fill, and every carriage in the last train out of Peterboro' was literally crammed with human beings: the rush at the station was so great that it was found necessary to admit persons by five at a time. Fortunately, no accident whatever occurred. The trains now run 8 times a day viz. at half past 7 and 10am, half past 2 and quarter past 6pm from Stamford; and at half past 8 and half past 11am, and half pact 3 and quarter to 8pm from Peterborough.

(SM 9 October 1846)

Despite the 'rain falling unmercifully', large crowds assembled to see the first train leave and on Sunday 'a dense crowd beset the station and thronged the line for a considerable distance.' (LC 9 October 1846).

Completion of the Eastern Counties Railway between Ely and Peterborough on 14 January 1847 enabled that company to take over from the London & North Western the working of traffic between Peterborough and Stamford together with the staffing of stations. Until this time a rail journey from Stamford to London involved changing to the LNW at Peterborough and proceeding via Northampton to Blisworth to connect with the main line to Euston. Now, an alternative route was available by the Eastern Counties from Peterborough via March, Ely and Cambridge to Bishopsgate station, London, an additional distance of four miles. The journey by the new route was expected to take thirty minutes less than via Blisworth, a promise that was frequently not fulfilled.

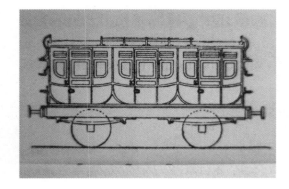

A Midland Railway Second Class carriage of 1848. Similar to a First Class in outward appearance, the seats were not upholstered.

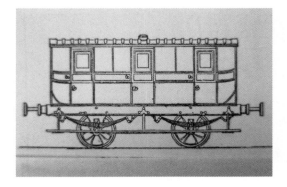

A Midland Railway Third Class carriage of 1848. The Railway Act of 1848 introducing 'Parliamentary' trains required something better than open trucks for Third Class passengers. Upholstered, there was no ventilation when the door windows were closed.

A correspondent warmly complains of the delays and want of attention on the part of some of the officers on the Eastern Counties railway. On the 21st inst. a respectable inhabitant of Stamford was waiting at Whittlesea to return by the train which should reach Stamford at 10 minutes to 9pm: he was at the Whittlesea station at 20 minutes to 8 but it was past 11 before the train arrived and an hour was occupied in travelling thence to Peterborough (6 miles). At the Peterborough station the passengers to Stamford were requested to alight from the carriages and get into those attached to the express train, which shortly after came up: they did so, and after seating themselves in the express carriages, were detained for nearly an hour and a quarter before the train left the station: to questions put by the weary travellers to the porters of the company and the engineers as to the reason of their being detained, either evasive answers or no answers at all were given; and in reply to earnest enquiries to speak to the station master the remark was 'He is not here'. On arriving at Stamford at half past three in the morning greater civility was shown as the station master and his assistants were in attendance to receive the train and every attention was paid to the speedy release of the passengers, some of whom had been 13 hours and a half in travelling 115 miles by rail. (SM 29 Jan 1847)

Provision of an alternative route from Stamford to London via March, Ely and Cambridge on the Eastern Counties from Peterborough, instead of the London & North Western via Blisworth, resulted in a reduction in fares.

	New fare	Previous fare
Single Ticket		
First class	15s	19s
Second class	11s 6d	14s
Third class	7s	7s 2d
Day returns		
First class	21s 6d	26s 6d
Second class	16s 6d	19s 6d

As might be expected, the new route abstracted traffic from the Peterborough-Blisworth line.

By August 1847 it was reported that increased charges for goods traffic by the Eastern Counties caused many Stamford tradesmen to have their supplies sent via the London & North Western to Sibson (Wansford) and then by road.

At Peterborough the Eastern Counties opened additional passenger facilities:

The refreshment rooms at the railway station here were opened for the accommodation of the public on Tuesday last; upon which occasion a sumptuous repast consisting of every delicacy of the season was provided and served up in first rate style by Mr. Biney, the worthy host of the Crown hotel and proprietor of the rooms. A numerous and highly respectable party did justice to the good things set before them; and the festive song was kept up with great spirit till next day's dawn. The rooms are very beautifully fitted up and are altogether a great addition to the station which may now be said to rank amongst the first in the country. (SM 2 July 1847)

The Eastern Counties announced the opening, on 21 October 1847, of a new cattle station at 'Helpstone' offering farmers in the grazing districts of Lincolnshire the advantage of the more speedy transit by rail to send their beasts to London, thus avoiding the loss of weight suffered by the animals when driven on the hoof. Although referring to a different route, the following complaint could no doubt be applicable to many rail journeys suffered by animals:

> A correspondent earnestly requests us to call attention to the serious losses farmers and graziers sustain by the mismanagement of the servants on the London & North Western Railway. It is stated to be no unusual occurrence for beasts and sheep to be at the station for 6 and 7 hours after the time of starting, and on their arrival at the London terminus be again detained for 3 or 4 hours before they are removed from the carriages, thus being unnecessarily kept for a long time in a state calculated to deteriorate their value in the market. 'But this' adds the correspondent 'is not the worst, for I understand that in some instances although the carriage has been paid, the cattle have not been delivered in time for the market as they ought to have been. The "Lords of the road" will scarcely deign to give one moment's consideration to such "trifling matters", and until some village Hampden shall step forward and teach them by the verdict of a jury that they are in the eyes of the law no more than common carriers for hire, and are liable to make good all the damage the owners may sustain by the loss of a good market, it is feared that the present state of things will not be remedied, unless indeed they should be shamed into a proper course by exposure in the public press.' (SM 29 January 1847)

Cooke & Wheatstone had invented the electric telegraph in 1843 and the railways were the first to make use of it. Peterborough was connected to London by telegraph over the London & Birmingham line from 1845.

The Syston & Peterborough Act required the Midland to install electric telegraph:

> And be it enacted, That the said Company shall and they are hereby required, or at any Time, on Receipt of a Notice to that Effect from the Lords of the Committee of Her Majesty's Privy Council for Trade and Foreign Plantations, to lay down and maintain along the whole or any Part of the Railway by this Act authorised to be made, as well as on the Line of the Midland Railway, an Electric Telegraph, of such Principle of Construction as shall be approved of by the Lords of the said Committee, which Telegraph shall at all Times thereafter be at the Disposal of Her Majesty for the Purpose of receiving and sending Messages, subject to such reasonable Remuneration for the Use thereof as may be agreed upon between the Lords of the said Committee and the said Company, or in case of Disagreement as may be settled by Two Arbitrators, to be named, the one by the President of the said Committee, and the other by the Directors of the said Company, and if such Arbitrators shall not agree, then by an Umpire, to be named by them before entering upon the Reference, and the Award of such Arbitrators or Umpire shall be conclusive on all Parties.

In January 1847 telegraphic communication between Stamford station and London direct was inaugurated. 'Telegraph House' in Wothorpe Road (known as Back Street at one time) was named the 'Telegraph Inn' from 1847 until 1961, which indicates the significance of this innovation to the town. In July 'railway time' was brought to Stamford:

UNIFORMITY OF TIME BY TELEGRAPH

The Electric Telegraph Company are now making such arrangements as will enable them to communicate the true time as observed daily at the Royal Observatory at Greenwich, to every station on the various lines of railway where the company has a telegraph station, and of course to all large towns throughout the kingdom. It is now the daily practice at Greenwich, at one o'clock, to indicate the true time by dropping a ball from the upper part of the observatory, which being telegraphed to the Admiralty and signalled to the shipping on the Thames, enables ships' chronometers to be adjusted. The contrivance by which the telegraphic company propose to extend the knowledge of this exact time throughout the kingdom is exceedingly simple. It is intended that the ball, immediately upon being detached at the top of its fall should strike a spring which, connected with the various lines of electric wires of the company will instantly strike a bell at every station. Thus it is not only possible and practicable, but what in all probability will be a matter of daily experience ere very long - that before the ball at Greenwich Observatory shall have reached the ground in its fall, the electric bell at Manchester shall have been struck and set ringing; so that we shall know it is one o'clock at Greenwich before the ball announcing that fact there has finished falling a few feet. In this way the true time at Greenwich will be kept by every railway company and every large town in the kingdom.

(SM 23 July 1847)

A Midland 0-6-0 goods engine No 312 designed by Kirtley and built in Derby in 1849.

(Arthur Jordan collection)

RAILS UNDER ST. MARTIN'S

Parliament's approval for a deviation of the line from the original proposal has already been referred to. Approaching Stamford from the west, and after crossing the meadows, the line would deviate near Nun's Farm, tunnel under High Street St. Martin's, passing the property of Mrs. Hibbins and part of Mr. Robertson's coach factory. Part of Mr. Phillips large malthouse would have to be demolished and the line would emerge near the Union house on the Barnack road. This would avoid crossing the Great North road on the level at the north end of the town bridge. The George close would be the site for a '... first class station ... including rebuilding... the bridge in such a style as should make it equal to the vast traffic which would have to pass over it.'

(SM 14 February 1845)

By August 1845 work had begun on the west side of Stamford including surveying the site of the new station, but in December a rumour was circulating to the effect that the course of the line might have to revert to that originally proposed along the north side of the river. It was feared that the Marquess of Exeter was unable to make the Midland company a clear title to the land required for the deviation:

> It is stated that the land in question forms part of a grant by the Crown to the Burghley family, which is held on condition that it be enjoyed by a widow or dowager of the house whenever such may exist. (SM 19 December 1845)

Nothing more was reported of this supposed difficulty, so perhaps it formed part of a bargaining ploy by which the Marquess offered to withdraw his opposition to the proposed line in return for a payment of £40,000 for certain property for which the Midland offered £30,000.

By May 1846, after the passing of the Act for the deviation in the House of Lords, contracts were invited:

> ... for the grand station in the George close which, it is stated, is likely to be an imposing edifice built of stone from the quarries of Mr. Clement Bland, of Frith Farm, and Messrs. Simpson, of Little Casterton. (SM 15 May 1846)

In the meadows, a little south-west of the present station, it was necessary to divert the river Welland and the soil removed from the new cut was used to make an embankment on which the railway line would be laid down. These works destroyed Stamford's bathing place so that a new one was required;

> A suitable spot may be found at the bottom of the George Close; but as it would be contrary to the provisions of the Improvement Act to use this place (it being within the prescribed distance of a public path) unless it be boarded in so as to render it comparatively private some expense and proper negotiations will be necessary to render it available. It is believed that the Syston & Peterboro' railway company might be induced to do something handsome towards the accomplishment of the object as it is owing to the construction of their line that the old bathing place has been made too public to be hereafter used with any regard to decency. (SM 19 March 1847)

PLAN OF ACTUAL LINE THROUGH STAMFORD
(DASHED LINE INDICATES TUNNEL SECTION)

A number of discoveries of archaeological interest were revealed during work in the vicinity of Nun's farm. There had been a Benedictine nunnery here founded in 1136 for 'forty holy virgins living regularly in religion and pure virginity'. Local interest in these discoveries was such that on Sunday evenings several hundred persons were there at one time. Discoveries included a beautifully preserved jet crucifix, several rings of gold and numerous skeletons.

Excavations on the east side of the town encountered strata of hard stone between 14 and 16 feet in depth. Whilst the stone could be used for building purposes, its removal resulted in a slowing down of progress. In the cutting leading to St. Martin's tunnel it was necessary to use gunpowder to blast a way through. However, by November, west of the station site, near Nun's farm, work on an embankment progressed at about fifteen feet per day fed by some thirty ballast wagons.

Numerous accidents and problems with both navvies and contractors will be dealt with in a later chapter, but it is interesting here to note the beneficial effect the construction of the railway had on local employment;

> The railway works on the west side of Stamford continue to employ an immense number of labourers, and thus in a great degree prevent the distress which is usually felt at this season of the year for want of outdoor employment. This week and last, in addition to those employed in excavating and banking, as many as 50 men and boys have been employed in breaking stones to be used to raise the level of the line

When the excavations from the west were nearing St. Martin's the same bed of stone that had been encountered on the east side was met with, consequently slowing down progress. In Church Lane a lodging house had to be demolished, which some local residents considered to be the welcome removal of a long-standing nuisance.

A section of Wothorpe Lane was closed in January 1847 whilst a temporary bridge was erected. Similarly on the east side, the road between Water Street and Barnack Road was temporarily closed until a stone bridge was completed in April 1847.

An example of the legal arguments which could and did develop concerning the acquisition of land or property by railway companies concerns Mrs. Hibbins. Her property in High Street St. Martin's, previously referred to, was the subject of an action in the magistrates' court when Mrs. Hibbins complained that the Midland Railway Company had not compensated her for tenant's rights in respect of her house and shop required for the construction of the Syston & Peterborough line of railway:

> It was stated that the parties could agree on all points except on the question which arose under the 121st section of the Act 8 Victoria C 18, whether a tenant in business be entitled to compensation for a period beyond which, under a notice to quit, the possession of premises ought to be given up. Mr. Thompson, in a lengthened argument, contended that such was the case; and that as Mrs. Hibbins' landlord (the Marquess of Exeter) it was well known did not usually disturb tenants who paid their rents and who therefore might calculate upon a long continued tenancy, she had a right to compensation for the goodwill of her business for a longer term than until the expiration of the legal notice to quit. She claimed to be so

considered under the words of the Act which allow magistrates to award compensation or any other damages, and those particularly enumerated. On the other side it was contended that, as Lord Exeter the landlord had, for a large sum of money, sold to the railway company all his interests in the property on the line, Mrs. Hibbins could not possibly have a right which had not been by that arrangement adjusted. The magistrates (four present) after much attention to the subject, were unanimously of the opinion that it was not in their power to award anything to Mrs. Hibbins on the principles set up. The applicants thereupon withdrew, and in a few minutes it was announced that £150 (which had been offered) would be accepted by Mrs. Hibbins for the loss she would sustain by being removed from her late shop and premises. (It is said she had demanded nearly ten times that amount.)

A similar claim was then introduced on behalf of Mr. David Davison who as subtenant holds a blacksmith's shop (part of the above premises) under Mrs. Hibbins. Mr. Davison required £40 for compensation for being disturbed before the expiration of a legal notice; the company offered him £20; the magistrates under all the circumstances (particularly his having paid £20 for goodwill on entering) thought £30 should be paid, and the suggestion was acquiesced in by both parties. (SM 29 January 1847)

William Bowker of Nun's Close, St. Martin's, was allowed £20 for damage with 50 shillings costs by the magistrates, as compensation for tenants in respect of injury sustained by him as a result of the railway's construction.

The importance the Midland Railway attached to the Syston & Peterborough line was in evidence when, in February 1847, the Chairman of the Company, George Hudson MP and Lord Mayor of York, arrived in Stamford accompanied by officials of both the Midland and the Eastern Counties companies. Concerned at the delay to the works due to difficulties encountered in the St. Martin's cutting it was decided to set on more labourers. At the time, High Street St. Martin's had not been reached and orders were given for the work to proceed by both day and night.

From the platform end can be seen Wothorpe Road bridge, Church Lane bridge and the mouth of the tunnel under High Street, St. Martin's (the Great North Road). Temporary wooden bridges carried these roads over the works while the railway was under construction.

(Robert Humm)

By mid-March half the carriageway in High Street St. Martin's was blocked and the other half carried over the excavations on a temporary bridge. Robertson's coach works in that street was temporarily removed to a site in Burghley Lane. The Midland was paying the proprietor £450 compensation for the inconvenience caused, and undertook to replace the house and warehouse upon arches over the railway within three months or forfeit a sum of money.

Beyond Nun's Farm the permanent rails had been laid for some distance and the embankment completed almost to Easton. On the other side of St. Martin's the excavations were impinging upon Barnack Road before running parallel with it towards the temporary station.

However, the danger from blasting with gunpowder in St. Martin's was causing concern:

> We have spoken before of the great danger to the public which proceeds from the bad practice of those engaged in cutting the line of railway through St. Martins, Stamford, in carelessly blasting masses of rock with gun-powder. Almost all the houses in the neighbourhood of the present workings have been riddled in their roofs by the descent of stones which have been thrown into the air by these explosions. On Tuesday last a stone weighing lllbs and a half fell through the slates and ceiling into the bedroom of Mrs. Barker's house, the property of Mr. John Lumby, in Water-street; and other persons' dwelling houses, as well as the large malting of Mr. Phillips in the same locality, have been repeatedly penetrated by similar missiles. Passengers in the neighbouring streets and roads incur almost as much hazard as if they illustrates the audacity and recklessness of the contractors for such works and shows the necessity of a vigilant attention to their proceedings   (SM 20 August 1847)

In March 1847 some surprise was expressed when the surveyor for the Midland intimated to the Stamford Improvement Commissioners that the new station might yet be erected near the temporary station at the east end of Water Street. This depended upon Earl Brownlow building a bridge over the river from his property in Brownlow Street, and whether the townspeople would prefer the station there rather than in the George close. Mr. Thompson, for the Commissioners, considered that a bridge at that end of the town 'would prove highly beneficial and is necessary in addition to the new bridge which is to be built on the old site'. Nothing came of this proposal, although the Albert bridge has spanned the river since 1863.

The Improvement Commissioners were understandably concerned about the provision of bridges over the new line and Mr. Liddell, the Midland engineer, promised that a bridge at the end of Water Street and another near the Sun public house at the corner of Church Street and Wothorpe Road, should be erected immediately. The Sun, which was renamed the Sun & Railway after the line had opened, was demolished in 1958 and the site is now Coulson's coal depot.

In the course of excavations in St. Martin's it was discovered that the stone was impregnated with oxide of manganese. The surveyor in charge of the works expressed the opinion that if manganese proved to be sufficiently abundant then it would be profitable for a company to be formed for its extraction. Nothing further was heard about this.

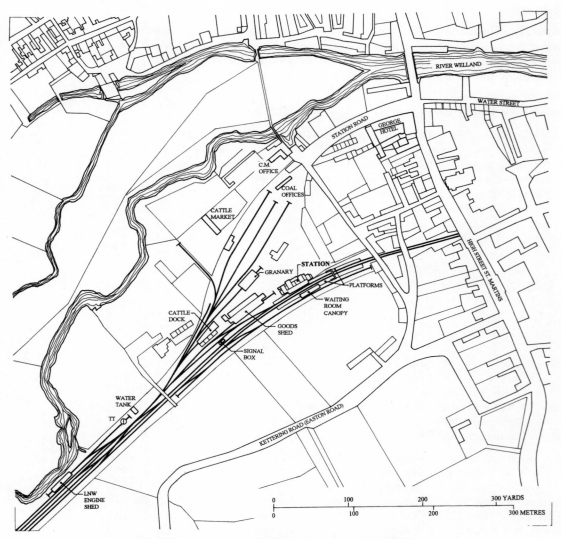

PLAN OF STAMFORD MIDLAND RAILWAY STATION

A HANDSOME NEW STATION

By May 1847 work had begun on levelling the George close ready for the erection of the station which, when he visited Stamford in February, George Hudson had promised would be one of the most elegant structures of the kind in the kingdom: 'the exterior would be in the Elizabethan style and assimilate in character to the architecture of Burghley House'. (SM 7 May 1847)

However, when the building of the station commenced in July, it seems that the company's plans were less ambitious:

> The building for the accommodation of passengers will not be so extensive as anticipated; but it will be a very handsome one and undoubtedly quite sufficient for the purposes intended. The buildings for the goods and engine department will be much more capacious. It is said that the Stamford & Rugby line will be opened before Christmas and that the station will be completed prior to the event.
>
> (SM 20 August 1847)

Although the temporary Stamford station at the end of the line from Peterborough had opened in October 1846, more than a year later the section on to Melton Mowbray was not completed. In December 1847 Stamford's permanent station was not ready although the main building had been roofed. Local tradesmen were complaining, particularly as the promise of cheap coal made more than two years earlier had not yet been fulfilled.

By March 1848 the permanent way was complete throughout from Syston to Stamford's temporary station and, of course, to Peterborough. Goods trains were run over the line thus helping to consolidate the trackbed, whilst the new goods station and coal depot at Stamford opened on March 20th. The Midland now took over from the Eastern Counties the working of the Stamford - Peterborough section.

May 1st saw the opening of the Syston & Peterborough line throughout by the completion of the missing link between Melton and Stamford. With the new station still not completed passenger trains were accommodated at the temporary station in Water Street. Probably because of the failure of the Midland to keep to its promises for earlier openings there were no civic dignitaries to welcome the first train, neither do Midland directors appear to have been present:

> The opening for passenger traffic of the Syston & Peterborough Railway took place on Monday last, though without any ceremony. Some of the tradesmen of Stamford had promised their assistants a holiday on the occasion but the very limited notice as to the opening (it having been announced only on Saturday) prevented any general arrangement, and for want of unanimity on the part of some of the drapers, none of the tradesmen in that line of business closed their shops. A few other tradesmen shut up at 12 o'clock and set their assistants and apprentices at liberty for the remainder of the day. The first train from Leicester, consisting of an engine and tender and four carriages, arrived at Stamford (a distance of 40 miles) in an hour and a half, and

BR Class 4 4-6-0 No 75061 on a Peterborough-Leicester train in 1963. Behind the brake-van is the goods shed; on the left the cattle dock; and behind stands the tall grain warehouse.

(P.H.Wells)

> nearly the same proportion of time was kept by the subsequent trains. One which arrived from Leicester about mid-day brought a band of musicians from Rutland: they proceeded to Peterborough and returned by the next train to Stamford where they alighted, and, playing through the town, imparted something like holiday strains to the inhabitants for three or four hours.   (SM 5 May 1848)

With the passage of trains through St.Martin's some residents found cause for complaint to the Stamford Improvement Commissioners that 'the steam, smoke and noise from the trains was a great nuisance to persons crossing the bridges'. In July 1848 the Clerk to the Commissioners was instructed to serve notice on the Directors of the Midland Railway calling on them 'to make a covering over the line from the tunnel in High Street St. Martin's to the entrance to their station in the George close'.

It would seem that the opening of the line throughout was not hailed as entirely successful by everyone. A correspondent in the Stamford Mercury in May 1848 wanted to know why the 10.10am from Stamford did not reach London via the Eastern Counties Railway until 4.20pm. A journey time of 6h 10m was $1^{1}/4$ hours longer than before the Syston & Peterborough line opened throughout, whilst the 1.20pm from Stamford took $6^{1}/2$ hours to reach London.

Shortly afterwards the Eastern Counties put on an 'express' train leaving London at 6pm and arriving in Stamford at 10.35pm. However, in July there were complaints that connections between the Eastern Counties and Midland trains at Peterborough were frequently missed because 'of lack of cordiality between the managers of the two companies'. (SM 28 July 1848)

The editor of the Stamford Mercury complained that fares were too high:

> The satisfaction which was felt at the opening of this important line of railway - connecting the eastern counties with the midlands and manufacturing districts - was

somewhat marred at the exorbitant fares to be charged as indicated in the timetable. The charge from Stamford to Melton, 22 miles by the old [turnpike] road, is 4s 9d in the second class, or at the rate of nearly $2^1/2$d per mile: the fare for the other classes is of course in proportion. This is, we believe, as high as the rate of charge upon any other railway whatever: it is more than double that upon either the Eastern Counties from Stamford to London or the North Western. The Directors will very soon find that in this part of the country low fares are the most remunerative.

(SM 5 May 1848)

At last, on Monday 23 June 1848, the new station was opened. This fine building, today Grade II listed, still fulfils its original purpose, except that the stationmaster's house now appropriately houses a transport bookshop. Designed by architect Sancton Wood, the builders were Groocock & Yates of Leicester who submitted a tender for £8,700.

It was earlier described as being in an Elizabethan style similar to Burghley House. The three-bayed loggia protects the entrance to the booking hall, with a ticket window originally on the right-hand side, the booking office having then been within the stationmaster's house. The waiting rooms, entered from the platform, have pointed windows and parapetted gables. The octagonal turret exceeds the tall chimneys in height and is surmounted by a weather-vane displaying the initials SPR.

In the turret was a bell tolled about ten minutes before the departure of a train. Few people carried pocket watches and Stamford's clocks were unreliable, as a correspondent to the Lincolnshire Chronicle complained:

… when will some plan be adopted for securing something like uniformity amongst Stamford's clocks? … Much stress is laid upon the advantage of the railway to this town… but what gain is the speed of a railway to the man of business, if by being misled as to the time, he miss the train he intends to go by … ?

(LC 25 September 1846)

This 1987 view of Stamford station shows the elegance of Sancton Wood's Tudor-style building somewhat marred by the platform canopy. The bell-tower and weather vane are prominent features.

(Robert Humm)

At the station, the original cast-iron columns still support a replacement canopy for that which, in its turn, must have replaced the 'galvanised iron roof' referred to just before the station opened. (LC 28 April 1848)The same paper considered that 'the public convenience appears to have been kept steadily in view throughout regardless of expense'.

What was for many years an island platform with a bay for the Seaton branch train, may originally have been a single-sided platform, because it was originally envisaged that the London & North Western would have its own station 'a short distance west of Nun's Farm …' (SM 30 May 1851) Facilities included a spacious goods yard with a goods shed. No longer required, the temporary station at the end of Water Street could now be dismantled for use elsewhere and the right of way to Hudd's mill restored to public use.

More than three months after the opening of the station the promised new road from the Town Bridge to the station had not been made. A Mr. Duncomb, baker, was an obstacle to progress on the road since he refused to give up the key to premises which he had vacated and which were to be demolished. He argued that as the Marquess of Exeter had received an extraordinary sum for the freehold, he (Duncomb) had a right to £500 'goodwill' compensation for quitting. The Midland resisted his claim, contending that Duncomb had moved from an old house on one side of the lane to a new house on the other side, and since his business faced no additional competition, the matter of 'goodwill' did not arise.

Constructing Station Road involved the demolition of the George's cockpit, an octagonal stone building said to be large enough to hold 500 people.

By 1850 Bradshaw's Railway Timetable showed departures for Peterborough at (arrival time in brackets) 7.35 (8.10); 9.43 (10.20); 1.50 (2.35); 4.55 (5.30); 9.45 (10.20). Sundays 10.44 (11.25); 8.10 (8.50). Only the 4.55pm conveyed third class passengers. Departures for Leicester were at 9am (11.05); 12.33 (2.35); 4.45 (6.43); 8.03 (10pm). Sundays 8.05 (10.20); 6.10 (8.25).

Bradshaw's timetable 1850

Fares were to Peterborough 2s 6d; 2s; 1s 3d. To Leicester 8s 6d; 6s 6d; 3s 6d.

A correspondent to the paper complained that 'There are five passenger trains up and down the Syston & Stamford new railway daily; but such is the independence of the company that they do not think it worth their notice to stop at intermediate stations for passengers more than twice a day'. An instance was given of over 100 persons at Luffenham and Ketton being disappointed when trains which would have taken them to Stamford market, did not stop. 'The directors are not aware that Stamford corn market does not commence until 2 o'clock, and does not finish until 4 o'clock, by which time farmers expect to have received their money from merchants and millers.'

An example of local enterprise meeting a need of railway travellers was that of a Stamford printer:

> Mr. Sharp, printer of High Street, has commenced supplying an article which was much wanted by railway travellers, viz: a table (published monthly) which shows at a glance the arrival and departure of trains at every place on the line, the fares, and distances from Stamford, and such other particulars as are generally found useful to passengers. The table of fares shows some curious inequalities; thus a traveller going 6 and a half miles eastward of Stamford (to Helpstone) is charged 1s 3d in the first class; but if he go only 6 miles westward (to Luffenham) he is charged 1s 6d.
>
> (SM 9 June 1848)

Later Mr Sharp advertised another service:

RAILWAY MAPS

> Parties desirous of having their old maps rendered complete with the additions of all the lines of Railroad laid down at the present time are respectfully informed that Mr. Stephen Sharp undertakes to introduce them correctly on any maps with which he may be entrusted, on reasonable terms.
>
> St George's-square, Stamford, September 28 1848

A passenger to Manton in August 1848 complained that rain poured through the carriage roof from the opening where the lamp ought to have been. On the same journey, a few days earlier, the lamp glass was broken and oil poured on to passengers. This correspondent also complained of unpunctuality, giving the example of a train 1 and a half hours late, during which time passengers at Manton, where there was no waiting shelter, were exposed to a thunderstorm.

During the four years in which the railway was under construction no start had been made on the construction of a new town bridge for which the Act required the Midland Railway to pay £5,000 to the Marquess:

> Whereas the said Railway is intended to cross the High street in the Parish of St. Mary Stamford near to a certain Bridge over the River Welland which is at present inconveniently narrow, and it is anticipated that unless such Bridge be widened great Inconvenience may arise from such crossing; be it therefore enacted, That the said Company shall and they are hereby required to contribute a Sum not exceeding Five thousand Pounds, or so much thereof as may be necessary, towards the widening of the said Bridge, if at any Time required to do so, within Twelve Months

after the passing of this Act, by the Owner or Owners of the said Bridge, or other the Person or Persons who may have Power and Authority to cause the said Bridge to be widened: Provided always, that the said Money shall be outlayed in widening the said Bridge to the satisfaction of the Engineer for the Time being of the said Company, and under his Superintendence or Control, and so as to allow of Carriages conveniently passing each other thereon, with proper Footways either Side: Provided also, that if the Owner or Owners of the said Bridge, or other the Person or Persons having Power to Authorise and direct the same to be widened, shall not cause the same to be so widened within Twelve Months after the passing of this Act, then and in such Case the said Company shall and they are hereby required to do and perform all necessary Acts for obtaining Authority from Parliament to widen the said Bridge, and on obtaining such Authority shall widen the same at their own Expense.

Congestion and its accompanying accidents and disputes continued. In April 1846 a small boy was seriously injured when crushed against the parapet of the bridge by a cart laden with wood. On another occasion the Marquess, on horseback, encountered the Nottingham mail coach which refused to give way to His Lordship even when the coachman was threatened with a riding whip. Sometime later the 'Red Rover' coach collided with the carriage of Mrs. Eaton of Easton-on-the-Hill resulting in the overturning of the stage coach.

Earlier, the Editor of the Stamford Mercury, in reporting a nasty collision, took the opportunity again to attack the Marquess:

STAMFORD BRIDGE AGAIN!

This disgraceful and dangerous passage was again the scene of obstruction and contention on Monday last. The Marquess of Exeter was not on this occasion personally concerned, but his carriage and some members of his family formed the aggression. A fly, closely followed by a gig in which was a lady seated alone, had arrived on the crown of the bridge from St. Martins when Lord Exeter's carriage approached from the opposite side and proceeded onwards until the horses heads of both vehicles nearly came in contact. The coachman of the Marquess and the driver of the fly stared spitefully at each other and neither seemed inclined to yield, when, to prevent a violent collision (the consequences of which might have been most awful) a person rushed to the head of the horse attached to the fly and commenced backing it, much to the alarm and terror of the lady in the gig, to whom some of the neighbouring inhabitants found it necessary to render assistance. In backing the vehicles the gig was nearly upset by being forced against some waggons laden with wood which were standing opposite the Anchor Inn. The confusion caused by the incident led to imprecations loud and deep on the head of the person who owns, and has refused to improve, the unsightly structure. It is indeed a crying grievance to all passengers that the Marquess of Exeter, for the sake of his pocket, should allow the bridge, for which he takes toll, to remain in its present condition, dangerous as it is to the lives and limbs of all who are compelled to make use of it. Should a fatal accident occur Lord Exeter will be as morally and legally liable to a heavy deodand as are the proprietors of railways for any loss of life caused by want of proper precaution and safeguards on their lines.   (SM 19 December 1845)

At last, in May 1846, it was known that Francis Giles, engineer, had been engaged by the Marquess to superintend the construction of a new bridge for which the architects were Edward and Henry Browning of Stamford. Robert Woolston of Stamford undertook the contract which eventually resulted in his bankruptcy.

Whilst the old bridge was demolished and the new constructed arrangements had to be made for the passage of traffic along the busy Great North Road:

> Considerable misunderstanding has taken place with regard to the construction of the road to be used during the pulling down and rebuilding of Stamford bridge. At first it was arranged that a temporary bridge should be erected across the Welland from Water street to Mr. Harper's wharf; but Mr. Harper, as the lessee of the river, claimed compensation, and failing to get what he considered an adequate sum he put a stop to the works. [A temporary footbridge was later erected.] Under the direction of the Marquess of Exeter or his agents, Mr. Woolston, the contractor, then commenced making a road in the meadows from the George bridge to the Castle dyke, but was again very soon stopped owing to interference on the part of the town authorities, in consequence of no arrangements having been made with reference to the maintenance of the wide bridges to be erected in place of the present footbridges leading into the meadows. For a week nothing was done; Mr. Woolston in the meantime being at great expense in keeping the men he had engaged for the work. On Friday last activity in the matter was again shown; and it was stated that the road would be made from a corner of the George close with a bridge across the Welland near to (but independent of) the parish bridge called the George bridge, and also another bridge at the side of the Lammas (corporate) bridge; but on Monday last the workmen were again at a standstill; the alleged reason being that the last plan had been commenced without Lord Exeter's sanction having been obtained. It is stated that the directors of the Syston & Peterboro' railway will interfere if the new high bridge be not speedily - commenced yesterday workmen were engaged in laying down soil for a road across the meadows. (SM 4 June 1847)

Demolition of the old bridge commenced at the end of July 1847 after which the Great North Road traffic to and from St. Martin's followed the diversion across the meadows, along Castle Dyke and into Sheep Market. By November the Stamford Improvement Commissioners were complaining that the temporary road across the meadows was in 'a foundrous state and if the weather should become alternately frosty and moist will soon be positively impassable'. In December the Welland was in flood:

> The thoroughfares from Stamford to St. Martin's are now, in consequence of a flood in the river Welland, in a most unsatisfactory state. The road across the meadows is almost a quagmire and the temporary wooden bridge from the wharf to Water street is unapproachable except by planks extending across the road. On Tuesday, before these planks were supplied, some railway labourers were in attendance for the purpose of carrying passengers from the road to the steps of the bridge: we hear that one man earned 3s by this novel employment, females being his principal customers. (SM 10 December 1847)

Contractor Woolston appeared before the Improvement Commissioners to give an assurance that, should the flood waters rise higher, he would be prepared with 'a raft, boats or anything to convey passengers and mails across'. In order to establish foundations for the bridge below the river-bed use was made of a coffer dam, a water-tight enclosure pumped dry to enable men to work below the waterline. Encountering unsuspected springs the coffer dam was repeatedly flooded, despite the use of a steam-powered pump.

By July 1848 contractor Woolston was bankrupt and Edward Browning took control, but still the work was dogged by failure of the coffer dam. An unnamed engineer of the Midland Railway considered that if that company had undertaken the building of the bridge it would have been completed four or five months earlier. The new bridge has three arches with cutwaters and solid parapets and is built with stone from Bramley Falls near Leeds. It was finally opened on 1 May 1849, but if the Marquess had hoped to make a profit on the £5,000 paid to him by the Midland Railway, he must have been disappointed, for it was estimated by 'those who pretend to understand such matters that the bridge will have cost upwards of £10,000 before it is finished'.(SM 13 December 1848)

Expecting to recoup some of this expenditure the Marquess had a toll house erected on the north-east end of the bridge. Local people resented paying tolls to cross this bridge and at least one riot ensued until, in 1868, the tolls were relinquished.

The tollhouse erected by the Marquess of Exeter at the north-east corner of the new bridge and which was a cause of protest and riot until collection of bridge tolls was abandoned in 1869.

(Elisabeth Jordan)

THE MISSING LINK IS FORGED

Whilst this book is principally concerned with the railway reaching Stamford, it is entirely appropriate to make some reference to construction of the Syston & Peterborough line on either side of the town. A detailed history of the whole line is a subject for another book.

In July 1845 surveying of the line between Syston and Melton Mowbray, $9^1/_2$ miles, was under way. The Midland was anxious to get this section opened by Christmas 1845 (only 4-5 months!) '... in order to afford the accommodation of quick transit to the sporting gentlemen at the beginning of the fox-hunting season'.(SM 25 July 1845) The 'sporting gentlemen' were to be disappointed because the line did not reach Melton until September 1846, and then only to a temporary station which was not replaced until May 1848. 'Mowbray' was added to the station name in November 1876.

At Oakham there was concern that the contracts awarded in 1845 did not include the section of line between Melton and Stamford. Two factors would result in this section not being opened until early in 1848; one was constructional problems, the other, Lord Harborough.

As originally projected the railway would pass through Lord Harborough's estate at Stapleford Park, but the Act afforded special protection for His Lordship's estate:

> Provided always, be it enacted, That nothing in this Act contained shall enable the Company to take or use any Part of the Park or Land enclosed as a Park, belonging to the Rt Hon Robert Earl of Harborough, situate in the Parishes of Saxby, Stapleford, and Wymondham, or either of them without, the Consent in writing of the said Earl, his Heirs or Assigns.

His Lordship exercised considerable influence over the affairs of the Oakham Canal, traffic on which would be adversely affected by the new railway. To overcome this the Midland Railway undertook to purchase the canal and to use parts of it for the new trackbed.

Opened throughout in 1803, the canal connected Oakham to the national waterways network via the Melton Mowbray Navigation. Fifteen miles long, it suffered frequent water shortages, in part due to his Lordship's refusal to allow steam pumping engines. A correspondent signing himself 'Civis Agricola' described it as '... a canal very inadequate to the wants of the county, with scarcely water enough in it to swim a goose, at one time dried up by the sun and at another time stopped by the frost'.(SM 31 January 1845)

Rarely paying a dividend above £2 on a £130 share until 1840 when £5 was reached, but by 1847 it was down to £3. Therefore the Midland Railway's purchase of the canal at £26,000 together with 200 newly created £40 shares in that company was most acceptable and was incorporated in an Act of July 27th, 1846.

Emerging from Manton Tunnel, about a century after its completion, a Class J39 0-6-0 No 64896 takes the Stamford line with a freight for Peterborough.

(Arthur Jordan collection)

This view from Saxby bridge shows the present track alignment whilst the 1848 curve followed the line of trees in the distance.

(Elisabeth Jordan)

His Lordship's refusal to allow railway surveyors to enter his land resulted in the 'Battle of Saxby'. The trouble began on 13 November 1844. A party of seven railway surveyors approached the canal towpath where they were met by a gang of estate workers who took them prisoner. They, together with their surveying instruments, were taken to Cold Overton Hall to appear before the magistrate, T.F.Turner. The magistrate being away, the prisoners were allowed to disperse for the night.

The following morning a renewed attempt by the surveyors was expected and by 9am about forty of the Earl's men were assembled at Saxby bridge to prevent any surveying. Next, an army of reckless-looking vagabonds, headed by representatives of the railway, arrived. Whilst lengthy negotiations took place between the solicitors from both sides Lord Harborough's men fenced-off the towpath with carts. With reinforcements on both sides the railway force prepared for another attempt but the County Police arrived and threatened to arrest anyone committing an assault. Both sides were advised to discard their weapons and to try their relative strengths by pushing, but to strike no blows.

On both sides some men were forced into the air and over the backs of others, some were pushed into the ditch, whilst all became covered in mud until the two sides could not be distinguished, much to the amusement of the spectators. The surveyors succeeded in getting their measuring chain onto the forbidden ground but the Earl's men grabbed it and, in the scuffle, it was broken.

On 16 November another attempt to survey was made even though solicitors for his Lordship had warned that a few cannon from his yacht would be in readiness! Again strong-arm forces from both sides were engaged in battle and once more the surveyors' chains and staves were broken. A case against the railway side was tried at Leicester Assizes on 26 March 1845 and resulted in a verdict of guilty of assault against all the defendants who were sentenced to one month's imprisonment and a fine of one shilling.

George Hudson M.P., Chairman of the Midland Railway Company.

(Illustrated London News)

A second case, Ward *v.* Lord Harborough, was an action for trespass, false imprisonment and damage to a theodolite. The jury found for the plaintiff and awarded damages of £8.

In spite of the Earl's opposition, the Syston & Peterborough Railway Act of 30 June 1845 sanctioned the line which would pass under his park by a tunnel. In October of that year George Hudson MP (The Railway King), Chairman of the Midland Railway, had a long interview with Lord Harborough at Stapleford Park endeavouring to effect an arrangement for the purchase of land required for the line but his Lordship adhered to the arrangement already made in the House.

The Parliamentary Committee of the House of Lords meeting on 22 May 1846 considered a second Syston & Peterborough Railway Act as it affected Lord Harborough's objections:

> The Select Committee of this Bill met today for the first time: the Duke of Richmond took the chair, and the members present were the Marquess of Ormond, Lord Blayney, the Earl of Uxbridge, and the Bishop of Chichester.

Mr. Austin, as Counsel for the promoters, recapitulated the progress of the Bill last year and Lord Harborough's grounds of opposition. In taking the present line by tunnel they passed the smallest segment of Lord Harborough's park at Stapleford and complied with the provisional clause enjoined by the Commons that no shafts should be sunk: the promoters put themselves to a cost of £30,000 by taking the present line which was suggested by his Lordship's agents. Mr. Whateley QC, objected to the tunnels passing the park in the manner proposed within a quarter of a mile of Lord Harborough's residence, and intersecting ornamental lodges, plantations and fish-ponds, which would render it intolerable. Mr. Liddell and Mr. Robert Stephenson, engineers for the promoters, deposed as to the practicability of the tunnel, and the impracticability of any other line: it would inflict little or no inconvenience upon Lord Harborough's property … Mr. Clayton, engineer and agent to Lord Harborough, gave evidence as to injury inflicted on the ornamental grounds. It might have been avoided by passing under a skirting plantation instead of under the park. The room was then cleared. On the re-admission of the public the Duke of Richmond said that the committee did not consider the damage to property sufficiently extensive to justify them in throwing out the Bill, but they should require the insertion of a clause to the effect that the line taken should be in conformity with the last proposal of Lord Harborough's agent and pass under the plantation instead of the park.

(SM 22 May 1846)

When eventually construction of the tunnel under Cuckoo Plantation began the roots of the trees above were destroyed and suddenly a large section of the works collapsed taking the trees with it. Since it was impossible to make the tunnel as sanctioned the engineers decided to form an open cutting. Lord Harborough objected to this and obtained an injunction preventing the making of the cutting. The railway company were thus at an impasse since it had powers to make a tunnel which could not be made, and at the same time preserve the trees, whilst there was now an injunction restraining them from destroying the trees or making an open cutting.

Consequently it was decided to make a deviation to the north, so avoiding the plantation entirely, but now his lordship obstructed the surveyors for the deviation and further confrontations between men of the two sides took place. In July 1846 the railway company indicted Lord Harborough and twelve other persons for conspiring to prevent Charles Liddell, and others from taking surveys and making plans and sections which 'had to be laid before Parliament, and for assaulting Charles Liddell and others. After five hours deliberations a jury at Nottingham returned a verdict of 'Not Guilty'.

This necessitated yet another Act of Parliament of June 1846 authorising the proposed deviation, after the railway had agreed to pay his lordship £25,000, but the additional works cost the company another £85,000. However, the 'Saxby Curve' would impose a severe speed restriction on the line until 1892 when it was re-aligned. A new Saxby station on the new line was opened in readiness for the Midland connection to the Midland & Great Northern line at Little Bytham in 1894.

Following the river valleys and the Oakham canal avoided the heavy civil engineering work involved if taken across the valleys and up, or through, contours of 220, 300,

400 and 450 feet above sea level. Utilising land owned by the Oakham canal avoided the need for fresh powers to acquire the land belonging to the Canal Company. The sinuous course adopted by the Syston & Peterborough line was explained by the Midland Chairman, George Hudson: 'I have always held that a line should bend to the population, and not leave the towns'.

In addition to the problems at Stapleford Park there were to be several other causes of delay in the construction of the Syston to Stamford section.

A tunnel 746 yards long was required at Manton and by July 1845 one thousand men were at work there and elsewhere along the line. The brick lining of the tunnel caused problems with resulting delay. At several places solid rock was encountered requiring the use of explosives resulting in numerous accidents to workmen. An experiment at Geeston, near Ketton, involved the use of gun-cotton instead of gun-powder for blasting rock and which the navvies considered to be superior.

OPENED THROUGHOUT

Although Oakham station was nearing completion, problems with Manton tunnel remained and there were several incomplete lengths of line.

It will be recalled that in 1844 George Stephenson had predicted that the line would be open within twelve months, of the passing of the Act, but now three years had elapsed and no-one yet knew when the promised 'boon of cheap coals will be experienced' at Oakham. The Midland Railway was also anxious to get traffic moving over the length of the line, having regard to the capital expenditure involved with little or no revenue being earned.

Stamford Midland Station in 1968. Roses still blossom in the station master's garden and curtains remain at the windows.

(Robert Humm)

In November 1847 consideration was given to erecting a temporary station on the east side of Manton tunnel to and from which passengers and goods would be carried by horse vehicles to Oakham, with the Oakham-Syston section being worked by locomotives. This proposal was not followed up.

An indication that the works might be nearing completion was an advertisement appearing in January 1848 for the sale of '30 very powerful and valuable draught horses' at Whissendine.

In February Mr. Ellis, Deputy Chairman of the Midland Railway, on visit to Stamford, promised that the line would open throughout on 1 March 1848, as Manton tunnel was completed and the unfinished section of line were in detached places and of very small extent. However after an inspection of the line between Syston and Stamford by a group of Midland Railway Directors on 20 February, the opening throughout was not thought possible before the end of March.

Another advertisement for the sale of contractor's equipment reinforced the hope that the works were nearing completion;

Manton, Rutland.

To Railway Contractors, Timber Dealers, Builders, Ironmongers, Plumbers and others.

Important sale of horses, machinery, foreign and English timber, lead and iron piping, wrought iron force pumps, etc.

J. Cooke is favoured with instructions from Wm. Worswick Esq., railway contractor, to sell by auction, on Thursday and Friday the 23rd and 24th days of March 1848, at Manton in the county of Rutland, 3 14-horsepower condensing engines with 18-horsepower boilers to each, suitable either for winding, sawing or grinding, with two sets of clay rollers and pugmill to each, in complete repair; claymill with pugmill constructed to work together; 2 claymills, two pugmills, force pump with 3 cylinders and engine for pumping water with piping 3ins in diameter and three-quarters of a mile in length; two miles in length of iron rails and chairs, about 5,000 yards of lead piping, force pump with brass cylinder, six lead pumps, six gins with horse arms, ropes and pulleys complete, 10,000 feet of 1 5/8 square best wrought iron, large cable chain, broad and narrow wheeled timber drugs, wheelbarrows, firebricks, ridge tiles, pantiles, etc, etc.

Also an immense quantity of memel timber, red and white wood, deals and battens, about 5,000 boards of inch deal, and an extensive lot of English timber which has been used in the building of Manton tunnel and was purchased by the present owner at a cost of more than £2,000, and the machinery and other effects at an outlay of upwards of £5,000. The whole is disposed of in consequence of the completion of the contract and will be sold in lots suitable to purchasers.

Also 14 valuable draught horses in first rate condition; brown horse by Wentworth, bay mare by The Count, two half bred horses, blood mare, three hackney horses and two ponies.

Also three 6-inch wheel carts, two 41-inch wheel ditto, 8 narrow wheel ditto, 30 sets of horse tackle, a number of horse cloths, patent chaff cutter, bean mill, two chaff boxes, etc.

Descriptive catalogues of the timber etc, also of the age, name and colour of the horses, will be ready 7 days prior to sale and may be had at all the principal inns in the counties of Leicester, Nottingham, Rutland and Northampton, and at the auctioneers office in New Street, Leicester.

Horses will be sold on Friday the 24th. Sale to commence each day punctually at 10 o'clock.   (SM 10 March 1848)

Charles Liddell, Engineer, J. F. Bell, Company Secretary and Capt. Symonds RE, Government Inspector travelled over the line on 27 April 1848 after which the opening was authorised. Oakham people gave the first train on May Day a rousing send-off:

On Monday last this town presented a scene of unusual activity on account of the opening of the Syston & Peterboro' Railway. The weather being fine and cheering numbers congregated at an early hour to enjoy the sight of the first passenger train. At 7 o'clock the Leicester and Peterborough trains met at our station and the attention of the porters and officers was put to the test as the rush upon both sides of the platform was great. At 8 o'clock the Oakham band played up the town to the station the 'Railroad Quickstep' and took their stand on the platform. At noon they entered the train for Stamford, when a rather laughable circumstance occurred: none of the second class carriages being large enough to hold the party, they got into a bullock waggon amid the jokes of the bystanders: however, they struck up 'Oh Dear What Can The Matter Be?' and this little incident caused much merriment.

(SM 5 May 1848).

Oakham people subscribed over £1,000 for the purpose of paving the causeway in each street with slabs. It was anticipated that this, together with the coming of the railway, would be 'the harbinger of extended trade and a large increase in visitors'.(SM 12 May 1848)

Completion of the line opened up possibilities for excursion traffic. When the Liverpool & Manchester Railway opened in 1830 excursion trains were run daily from both Liverpool and Manchester to the Sankey Viaduct, midway along the line. From then on railway excursions became a feature of most railways although, as we explain in our book 'Away for the Day' (Silver Link), it was the Great Exhibition of 1851 which encouraged an explosion of excursion trains until the Railway Times described the whole country as being 'alive with excursion trains'.

The name synonymous with 'excursion' is Thomas Cook, founder of the travel organisation which still bears his name although now in German ownership. Although not the FIRST railway excursion, the success of his temperance trip from Leicester to Loughborough in 1841 over the Midland Counties Railway encouraged Cook to develop the organisation for which he became famous. The Midland Railway embraced the Midland Counties and its excursion tradition so they, together with the Eastern Counties Railway, another of Hudson's lines, ran excursion trains from their formation.

In August 1847 it was announced that:

> ... a train would leave Wisbech on Monday morning at 1/4 past 8 on an excursion to Stamford, which will afford an opportunity of visiting Burghley House; and as the fares are fixed at a low rate it is anticipated a considerable number will avail themselves of this variation in the style of the trips which have hitherto been confined to steam vessels.

> The train is to return at 1/4 past 6.

About 100 people took advantage of this trip. Shortly afterwards the Midland, Eastern Counties and North Norfolk railways announced an excursion from Stamford to Norwich, Yarmouth and Lowestoft:

EASTERN COUNTIES AND NORFOLK RAILWAYS
PLEASURE EXCURSION TO NORWICH YARMOUTH AND LOWESTOFT

A train will leave Stamford, Peterborough and the undermentioned stations on Saturday the 14th of August 1847 as follows:

Fares to Norwich, Yarmouth, Lowestoft and back from

		First Class	Covered Carriages	Open Carriages
Stamford at	11.25	14s 6d	9s 6d	7s
Helpstone	11.36	..	..	..
Peterboro'	12.00	13s 6d	9s	6s 6d
Whittlesea	12.14	13s	8s 6d	6s
Wisbech	12.10	..	..	..
March	12.30	12s	8s	5s 6d

Arriving at Norwich at 4.45pm, Yarmouth 5.30pm, and Lowestoft at 6pm.

N.B. The tickets will be available for the return journey up to and including Saturday the 21st of August by the train leaving Yarmouth at 5 o'clock in the evening, Lowestoft at 4.30pm and Norwich at 6 o'clock. Tickets may be had at any of the above mentioned stations on and after Thursday the 12th inst.

By order, August 2nd 1847

(SM 13 August 1847)

It seems that the weather on the previous day put many people off this trip but those who went enjoyed 'an exceedingly pleasant journey' of 230 miles return for three farthings a mile first class. One surprise for Stamford folk was the price of bread in Yarmouth shops, being $2\frac{1}{2}$ d per 2lb loaf, whereas at Stamford the price was 6d per 4lb loaf.

An artist's impression of Thomas Cook's first excursion from Leicester to Loughborough in 1841. The locomotive depicted is a Bury 2-2-2 of the Midland Counties Railway.

(Arthur Jordan collection)

In September 1847 a special train, for which the 'new saloon carriage has been engaged', took the Commercial Cricket Club and a large party of supporters from Stamford to Wisbech for a return cricket match.

An attempt was made to develop Stamford and Peterborough as excursion venues for people from midland towns:

The Midland Railway Directors have announced that an excursion train will visit Stamford and Peterborough on Monday next. At Syston trains from Leicester, Derby and Nottingham will unite and form one train on the Peterborough line. The attractions at Stamford are held out to be the model of a fine old English town, the adjacent scenery and Burghley house and park; at Peterborough the Cathedral. The fares, which are exceedingly low (4s for the journey from and back to Leicester, and 4s 6d from and back to Derby and Nottingham) will most likely tempt an immense number of persons to leave those populous towns on a visit to a district noted for the richness of its sylvan scenery. It is probable that a cheap excursion train will run from Peterborough and Stamford to the Midland towns above mentioned. On the occasion of Leicester fair when an excursion train was started (although very little publicity was given to the arrangement) several hundreds of persons were conveyed from Stamford and Rutland stations. The trains from Nottingham, Derby and Leicester on Monday next will arrive at Stamford at 1/2 past 8am and leave at 1/2 past 7pm.

(SM 2 June 1848)

Eleven hours in Stamford did not prove the attraction anticipated, for only about 100 people alighted from the excursion train. About the same number went on to Peterborough where the benefit clubs were parading with a band. Of course, working people could not avail themselves of an excursion on a Monday so that the appeal could only be to the so-called 'better class of excursionist'.

A Whit Monday excursion to London from Oakham and Stamford reached its destination in 6 hours. It was a stormy day and, on the return journey 'the managers of the railway showed a liberal and conciliatory spirit' so that 'passengers who had tickets for the open trucks were not compelled to travel in that exposed manner but were accommodated with covered carriages'. (SM 16 June 1848)

Excursionists, even farmers and gentry, were not deterred by an early start, as this advertisement proves:

MIDLAND RAILWAY
ROYAL AGRICULTURAL SHOW AT YORK
Thursday July 13th 1848.

A special train will leave Peterborough for York on Thursday 13th of July taking up passengers at stations as under:

Leave Peterborough at 3am; first class 57s 8d; second class covered or open 43s 3d

Leave Stamford at 3.30am; first class 53s 8d; second class covered or open 40s 3d

[Also from Ketton, Luffenham, Manton, Oakham, Wymondham (renamed Wissendine from September 1848), Melton, Brooksby and Syston]

Return tickets will be granted for first class and second class in covered or open carriages, with which passengers may return by special train leaving York at 7.35pm the same evening, or by any train stopping at the above stations on the next day except the express leaving York at 3.55pm or the mail at 7.30. An early application for tickets is requested as places cannot be guaranteed after Tuesday the 11th inst.

By order, J. F. Bell, Secretary, Derby, July 4th 1848
(SM 7 July 1848)

About twenty carriages were required to convey excursionists from Peterborough, Stamford and Oakham to Leicester for a balloon ascent although it was suspected that the low fare of only 3s 6d for a journey of 80 miles was the main attraction. The balloon ascent was disappointing, being less than expected and it came down at Snibston.

Poor public relations lay behind the failure of an excursion train from Stamford to Norwich to attract more than seven passengers. It was said that the only announcement of the trip was by a few handbills the day before, 'not one person in fifty knew anything about it. People want more than 24 hours to make up their minds for a long holiday journey'. (SM 1 September 1848.)

By the time of the Great Exhibition of 1851 Stamford had the choice of four routes to London: the Midland via Leicester; via Rugby and the London & North Western; the Midland via Peterborough and the Great Northern; or by road to Wansford station for the LNW via Blisworth.

A year before the Exhibition a Stamford Provident Society was formed for the accumulation of funds 'to enable mechanics and others of Stamford and its neighbourhood to visit the "Great Exhibition of Industry of All Nations" by paying weekly small sums of money'.(SM 3 May 1850) Some were disappointed:

Some of the 'knowing ones' have been sadly taken in during the last week. Contemplating a cheap trip to see the World's Fair they obtained tickets from the Provident Society at Stamford with the intention of starting from Seaton or Rockingham stations and they are now informed that the tickets are of no use and that they will not be recognised by the persons in charge of those stations.

(SM 11 July 1851)

Large numbers of Stamford people took advantage of the cheap fares offered, most opting to travel by the LNW route via Rugby. The Stamford Gas Company arranged for their employees to visit 'The Crystal Palace' and made a contribution towards their expenses. Intending visitors to London were given a timely warning:

Persons travelling into or out of London by railway are cautioned against sets of card-sharpers who take daily excursions into the country for the purpose of entrapping the unwary.

The grain warehouse
of 1851 seen here in
1968 shortly before
demolition.

(Robert Humm)

COAL, CORN AND FISH

By the mid-eighteenth century dwindling woodlands and the growth of towns and cities had increased the need for coal. The principal source of coal for London, and most towns on a navigable river, were the collieries of the North East, in the Newcastle-on-Tyne and Stockton-on-Tees area. This 'sea coal' was carried in 'colliers', sailing ships plying between the northern ports and river estuaries along the east coast as far south as London.

From the 1660s Stamford had been supplied with 'sea coal' via the Wash, the River Welland, and the Stamford Canal from Market Deeping. As much as 3,800 tons a year reached Stamford wharf after a four day journey from Fosdyke. Surrounding villages and small towns as far as Uppingham and Oakham had benefited from this source of coal. The alternative of obtaining supplies by road from collieries in Leicestershire and Warwickshire was prohibitively costly for most people. For example, in the hard winter of 1844-45 the waterways froze-up forcing the Stamford gas works to obtain coal by road from Leicestershire at 11s 8d per ton, on which the carriage was 20s per ton.

Canals enabled coal to be conveyed at lower cost to most towns situated on contours accessible by the use of locks. Improvements to the River Wreake, known as the Melton Mowbray Navigation, and construction of the Oakham Canal gave Oakham, Uppingham and surrounding villages access to coal from Midland collieries. However, the Oakham Canal was frequently without water and coal supplies were held up for weeks on end. Supplies to Stamford, along its canal, also became increasingly unreliable.

Railways, not so dependent on the weather and able to reach almost all parts of the country, lowered the price of coal as well as maintaining regular supplies. Railway promoters made much of this advantage. George Hudson, Chairman of the Midland Railway, at a meeting of his Board in 1845, said 'The Syston & Peterborough line, which the Company propose to construct ... will reduce the cost of coal 50% in the eastern district'.

In December 1846, with the line open between Stamford and Peterborough, officials of the Eastern Counties Railway, which had not yet reached Peterborough, informed the Stamford 'authorities' that coals would be conveyed by that railway to Stamford and 'cold at a price considerably below that which has hitherto been known here'. The coals would be 'sea-borne from the north and freighted from the Thames up the river Lea to Stratford-le-Bow where they would be transferred to railway wagons for conveyance to Stamford. Prospects of competition in the supply of coal were opened up:

> It seems probable that there will be in future considerable competition in the coal traffic at Stamford and that the public will be supplied by a different class of persons than those who have hitherto carried on the trade. Since the announcement that the

This late 19th century view from the granary roof shows the Stamford Midland station coal yard. The line of coal offices with tall chimneys was demolished in 1994. The cattle market had not yet been moved from Broad Street at the time of this picture.

(Lincolnshire County Council: Stamford Museum)

Eastern Counties Railway Company had determined to convey coals along the line there have been numerous applications at the Stamford station relative to the rate of charges and the wharfage accommodation; and it is understood that several tradesmen, such as druggists, drapers, grocers and maltsters etc, are entering into arrangements to deal in the article. Among those most earnest in the matter, we have heard of Mr. Handson, Mr. Jelley, Mr. Rd. Knight, Mr. Tebbutt and Mr. Rogers. Part of the supplies are expected from Lynn by the way of Ely, but it is thought that the greater portion will come from the Thames along the Blackwall and Stratford line. It seems that coals unshipped at Blackwall avoid the London Port dues, which are exceedingly heavy, and thus Wall's-end coals can be sold in Stamford at a lower price than in the Metropolis, although the colliers bringing them reach within 10 miles of London. It is calculated that Yorkshire coals may be delivered here for 17s or 18s a ton, and Newcastle for 21s or 22s. The trade in Leicestershire and Derbyshire coals will be almost destroyed until the railway be opened from Stamford to Syston, as at present the small dealers are giving nearly as much for those coals at Oakham and Market Overtone as a better sort may shortly be purchased for at Stamford. The supplies expected by railway last week did not arrive; owing, it is said, to some misunderstanding or want of proper arrangement between the dealers here and the factors at Lynn and Ely. We hear that there is no obstacle on the part of the railway company to an immediate and regular conveyance of coals. The present inclement weather is causing the article to be very dear so that the new speculators are injuring themselves by delaying to pursue their project. (SM. 18 December 1846)

Not until February 1847 did the first coal by rail, 70 tons, arrive at Stamford's temporary station. The delay was attributed to the 'great scarcity of coal ships and river craft'. It was reported that many Newcastle colliers had been taken off coal-carrying to replace coasters which had been sent to America for the conveyance of corn which was almost certainly intended to relieve the Irish potato famine.

Owing to this diversion of shipping '... Messrs. English, of Wansford, who contracted for the supply of coals to the poor of Stamford, (the funds for which were raised by subscription) have been unable to effect deliveries at the periods expected.' (SM 22 January 1847)

When the first rail-borne coal arrived Messrs. Handson & Knight, the new coal merchants, offered a reduction of several shillings per ton from previous prices. It was believed that in the summer Sunderland coals would be available at 18s per ton against the prevailing price of 23s.

By April it was reported that coal traffic by rail to Stamford was increasing considerably and that, in addition to sea-borne coal, supplies were also being obtained from Clay Cross and other Derbyshire collieries. George Stephenson, the railway engineer, owned the Clay Cross collieries.

Since the Syston to Stamford section of railway was not yet completed, Derbyshire coal had to be routed over the Midland line to Rugby, then London & North Western via Blisworth to Peterborough, before being handed back to the Midland to reach Stamford. Needless to say, this circuitous route added to coal prices, but it was confidently believed that once the Syston-Stamford line was opened then the price of coal could be only two-thirds the present price.

In March 1848, with the line opened throughout for goods and traffic, this advert appeared:

STAMFORD COAL COMPANY

Handson, Knight & Co. beg respectfully to inform their friends and the public that they now have on sale at the Stamford station best Swanwick coal (for which they are sole agents), best hard pit coal from 13s 6d to 14s 6d per ton; Clay Cross coal 14s; cobbles from 9s 9d upwards. 1s per ton charged for delivery in the town. The above company ensure to the public full weight and do not intend to allow themselves to be undersold. (SM 31 March 1848)

These prices must be compared with the 23s per ton charged for sea-borne coal twelve months earlier.

Several coal merchants established stacking sites and offices at the new station and, from time-to-time, disputes arose; Edmund Chester, coal porter, was convicted of assaulting Mr. Samuel Clay, coal merchant, at Stamford station. A dispute had arisen regarding the right to deposit coals. Coal depots were opened at stations along the line as this advert shows:

MIDLAND COUNTIES RAILWAY
The Coal Trade, Luffenham Station.

Messrs. Betts & Hawley, having intimation from their friends that the Luffenham station is a convenient coal station for them, have at once arranged to deposit coal there and will endeavour to oblige to the utmost of their power all with whom they may have the honour of transacting business.

Luffenham station, October 18 1848

The coal trade is carried on
At Oakham station	)	
At Manton station	)	by Betts & Hawley
At Luffenham station	)	
At Stamford station	)	
At Ketton station	)	by G. H. Betts

G. H. Betts and Betts & Hawley advise their friends not to depart from the usual custom of laying in stocks of coal at this season. Coal MAY be dearer during the winter, it CANNOT BE CHEAPER. (SM 27 October 1848)

In January 1850 Ellis & Everard opened a coal depot at Uffington station 'for the sale of coal and lime of the best quality.'

With the Great Northern's Towns line planned to cross the Welland at Tallington in 1852, Messrs. Handson & Knight secured a lease of the Stamford Navigation with a view to establishing a water-rail coal transfer wharf at Tallington. In 1853 the Great Northern sought Parliamentary powers to construct a short canal from the railway at Tallington to the Navigation but this was defeated by the Earl of Lindsey.

Lower transport costs for coal reduced the price of gas in Stamford from 10s per thousand feet in 1847 to 6s in 1853 and 5s 6d in 1858.

Almost all aspects of life in Stamford were affected by the coming of the railway, in particular trade. The town, at the heart of an agricultural district and on a principal drove road for cattle from Scotland, had long been noted for its cattle fairs. The facilities offered by the railway for speedier transit both to the fair and to the farms and premises of buyers, as well as making it easier and more comfortable for farmers and dealers to travel to the fair, increased the numbers of both cattle and people attending:

Yesterday's fair for horned and polled cattle was the largest ever known. On Tuesday and Wednesday there were arrivals at the villages and inns in the neighbourhood from almost all the northern parts of the Kingdom: they came by rail as well as by road and many of the lots were accompanied by Scotch and Irish drovers. On Wednesday 200 beasts reached Stamford direct from Glasgow and yesterday morning a train has brought trucks filled with livestock. It is impossible to judge accurately of the number of beasts offered for sale but they were supposed to amount to between 12,000 and 15,000, or three times the average number exhibited at Smithfield market on any day during 1847 … A calculation was made that there were 1,500 beasts in Broad street, 800 in Scotgate, 300 in High street, 600 in Red Lion square, All Saints place and Barn hill, 100 in Ironmonger street, 150 in Sheep market etc. There was an abundance of buyers but they took advantage of the extraordinary supply to manifest a shyness in offering: the sellers however generally refusing to give way, sales at length became pretty brisk and some thousands changed hands at prices a trifle below those obtained at recent fairs. (SM 10 November 1848)

One might have expected the cattle market to have been located near the railway much earlier than 1896 when it was moved out of Broad Street to its present position.

Stamford's corn market, which ranked fourth in the country after London, also benefited from the railway, since factors from further afield could now attend. In August 1848 factors from Macclesfield and Manchester were noted among those arriving by rail. The electric telegraph, available at the railway station, enabled speculators to keep informed on price movements. By 3pm they had obtained information of the great advance on wheat prices at that day's market in Mark Lane, London. (SM 7 May 1847)

A prominent feature of Stamford's Midland station for over a hundred years was a large grain warehouse erected in 1851 and firm evidence for the importance of the railway to agriculture and the corn trade. Another well-known extant feature of the Stamford station scene, the bridge over the line to Nun's Farm, was erected in 1851.

New industries were established to serve the surrounding agricultural district but the railway gave access to wider markets. A brass and iron foundry was established by J. C. Grant in 1845 producing agricultural implements. Henry Smith had founded a farm machinery business in 1837, a firm which was eventually known as Blackstone's. Later producing portable steam engines, mostly for farms, these were distributed by rail. Smith's haymaker, chaff cutter and a horse rake sent to the Great Exhibition in 1851 gained a prize medal.

In Scotgate, Hayes & Son had a waggon and carriage business exhibiting its vehicles at shows around the country.

Opening the Syston & Peterborough line made Stamford engineering products widely available and steam-powered machinery, together with supplies of coal with which to fuel the engines, transformed agricultural production throughout the land. As well as opening the whole country to Stamford products, the town gained improved access to the those of other towns and districts.

This view shows the extensive timber yard which spread on both sides of the station approach road. The 'Sun and Railway Inn', on the corner of Church Street, can be identified in front of St Martin's Church.

(Lincolnshire County Council: Stamford Museum)

From Wisbech, via the Eastern Counties and Midland railways, a trader regularly brought to Stamford market large quantities of rhubarb and asparagus. In June 1847 he had the town crier announce that he would sell at his stall good bread at 1d per 4lb loaf cheaper than that charged by Stamford bakers. The train bringing the loaves was late but on its arrival 200 loaves were quickly sold, 'the people being so clamorous that it was with difficulty the bread could be weighed and pieces cut from other loaves to make up any deficiency.' However, this trade was not all one way because the man purchased 70lbs of butter and a large quantity of eggs to sell in Wisbech, where he said there was a ready sale. (SM 18 June 1847)

> Rail links to the North and East coasts made available in Stamford a daily supply of fish and at competitive prices:

> > The advantage of railways in equalising the price of provisions throughout the country has been demonstrated in Stamford during the last few days by the arrival of liberal supplies of Tweed salmon and salmon trout which has been disposed of by the fishmongers at a low price. This description of fish is despatched from Berwick at 6 o'clock in the evening and arrives at Stamford at 10 o'clock the next morning; and it is of course supplied to the public in very fine condition. (SM 7 July 1848)

The impact of the Great Northern Railway on both Stamford and the Syston & Peterborough line is dealt with elsewhere, but here it must be noted that its Loop line which was opened in 1848 connected Lincoln, Boston, Grimsby and the farmlands of the Fens with Peterborough and so with the Midland line to Stamford and beyond.

British Rail Standard Class 5 No 73137, with Caprotti valve gear, takes water before entering the tunnel under St. Martin's which caused considerable trouble at the time of its construction. The train was a Yarmouth special taking this route after the closure of the Midland & Great Northern line in 1959. On the building above can be seen the sign of the 'Telegraph Inn' which closed in 1961, a year after this picture was taken.

(P.H. Wells)

THE NAVVIES - I

Like all railways the Syston & Peterborough was not constructed without many casualties among the workmen, the navvies. An early fatal accident occurred near Melton Mowbray in February 1846 when a tip driver, in checking a horse which was slipping on wet sleepers, fell and was dragged five yards. He was taken to Leicester Infirmary with injuries to his foot where he died from lockjaw.

Although there were no fatalities several men were seriously injured in an accident near Bainton:

> A rumour of a painful nature was circulated in Stamford, on Saturday afternoon last, to the effect that several persons had been killed near Bainton, on the works of the Syston & Peterborough railway. On enquiry, it turned out that a very serious accident had occurred, but fortunately without occasioning any loss of life. It seems that a party of about 20 workmen had gone with several waggonfuls of rails to Uffington, and having unloaded were returning the empty trucks, propelled by the engine which had been recently placed on that portion of the line: on arriving at the road leading from Tallington to Bainton (the train progressing at about 12 miles an hour) the foremost waggon, on the oscillating motion of an empty body moving at such speed, got off the line: succeeding wagons were immediately dragged off also, and falling one upon the other, the men were thrown out and dreadfully crushed. The engine fortunately maintained its position on the rails. The engineer states that the progress of the train was obstructed by a large piece of wood, but the men declared that they saw no such obstruction, and that there were watchers on the line to remove any impediment. Ten of the men were severely hurt: three were without delay conveyed to the Stamford infirmary where they received prompt surgical assistance: one of them, John Whyman of Peterborough, was found to have sustained a compound fracture of the leg; the second, Henry Webbe of Nunton, also had a compound fracture of the leg; and the third, John Lieven of West Deeping, had a severe lacerated wound in one of his thighs. They are now doing well and likely to recover. The other men, though much bruised, were not so severely injured as to make their conveyance to the infirmary necessary: they were taken to public houses in the neighbourhood.   (SM 29 May 1846)

The Midland Railways inspector of the works at the Peterborough end was instructing a workman in driving a stake when the end of the mallet flew off, striking the inspector's head which was severely cut, endangering his life. In the same week of June 1846 a navvy died after he had one of his thighs crushed between two ballast wagons at Woodstone, near Peterborough.

Many risks were taken by navvies, some inevitable from the nature of their work, others resulting from their desire to earn as much money as they could. An accident at Morcott in December 1846 occurred as a man was removing wagons from a 'drag' when one of the supports slipped and fell on him. All his ribs were fractured and his lungs seriously damaged. 'The poor fellow, whose groans were terrific, was released as soon as possible ... Hopes are entertained that he will recover.' (SM 18 Dec 1846)

'Undermining' was the accepted process for dislodging large quantities of rock or spoil in cuttings. Frequently the undermining was taken too far and men were trapped beneath the collapsing mass. Such an accident occurred near North Luffenham on Good Friday 1847 when a man's injuries resulted in his death. A similar collapse of earth, eight feet in height, killed a man working between Ketton and Collyweston in July 1847.

Not all navvies came from distant parts, for many local men were engaged upon the work. Thos. Crowson of Duddington and Jas. Dye of Ketton were injured at Geeston by a large mass of stone dislodged when a charge of gunpowder exploded prematurely.

Yet another accident occurred at Geeston when a large rock from an explosion struck a navvy and fractured his skull, an injury from which he subsequently died. A 'tip horse' driver was the victim of an accident between Oakham and Ashwell:

> A serious accident has happened on the Syston & Peterboro' line of railway between Oakham and Ashwell, to a young man named John Lank, a native of Aslackby near Falkingham. He was employed with a horse to drive the waggons laden with earth and to tip them: whilst in the act of doing so, the horse going at full speed, one of his feet struck against a piece of clay and he fell across the railing: the wagon passed over one of his legs smashing it in a dreadful manner. He was immediately conveyed to his lodgings at Whissendine where he was attended by three surgeons who agreed that it was necessary the fractured limb should be amputated. This was done by Messrs. J. E. Jones and H. Douglas, who placed the unfortunate man under the influence of ether, and such was its effect that the patient was quite unconscious that his leg had been removed till some time after the operation had been satisfactorily performed. He is in a fair way of recovery. (SM 23 April 1847)

Loss of a leg was the price paid by a navvy on the works at Cord Hill near Wymondham, when he was 'running in' a tip waggon for his own amusement. Two accidents occurred on the same day near Stapleford Park, one to a workman, the other to a horse. The man was working on 'tipping', when he slipped and his foot was crushed between the wagon and the 'bumper.' The horse, which was pulling a tip-wagon over 'pile-bridge' in the Park, took fright at the sight of a locomotive, jumped over the bridge, fell 37 feet and was killed.

An inquest held in Stamford Town Hall drew attention to the appalling conditions under which some families lived:

> On Saturday evening last an inquest was held at the Town hall, Stamford, on the body of Sarah Beavis, aged 32, wife of a railway labourer, who died suddenly on the previous afternoon. She complained of being unwell in the middle of the day and went to lie down; about 5 o'clock she was found to be in a dying state and Mr. Hatfield, the surgeon, was sent for, but before he could arrive the woman was dead. Beavis, the deceased and their four children lived in wretched state in one of the rooms of a small house in Scotgate occupied by Edward Downes: they had scarcely any furniture, they slept upon straw, and their only covering at night was the

clothes they wore. Beavis himself had been unwell for some time which straitened their circumstances, though it was said they had not been in want of food. Mr. Hatfield was of opinion that death proceeded from natural causes, probably from the rupture of a small blood vessel, and a verdict to that effect was returned. Mr Wm Richardson, the foreman of the jury, induced his fellow jurors to give their fees to Beavis. (SM 18 February 1848)

There was no free health service available to injured navvies and doctors would only attend an accident if given a written order from the contractor. This made the contractor responsible for the doctor's charges. Disputes arose, one such being brought before Oakham County Court in February 1848. Mr. Jones, surgeon of Oakham, claimed £13 18s from a contractor named Williamson in respect of attendance, medicine and appliances administered to persons in Williamson's employment and at his request. An argument developed as to whether Mr. Jones was legally entitled 'to recover as a surgeon, he being without any specific qualification other than antiquity of practice.' Plaintiff was awarded the amount claimed plus costs. (SM 18 February 1848)

One of the governors of the Stamford Infirmary, in a letter to the local paper, complained of the cost of caring for injured navvies:

> … many of them have required extraordinary allowances of wine and other support, which has been most liberally afforded them; thus causing a great expenditure of the funds of an institution which was established to give relief to the poor of an agricultural district. The Midland Railway directors had been written to on the subject but their response was an annual subscription of only 5 guineas, whereas the cost to the Infirmary was already six times that amount. (SM 20 November 1846)

A navvies' tip-wagon and horse. Pulling the loaded wagon to the edge of an embankment, both man and horse would deftly step aside allowing the wagon to bump against a stop-block thus causing the wagon body to tip forward shooting its contents out.

(Arthur Jordan collection)

A contractor's engine stoker was killed near Saxby bridge when he slipped as he descended from the locomotive and one leg fell across the rail. A wheel severed his leg and his abdomen was struck by a piece of metal beside the rails. He received no treatment until reaching Leicester Infirmary twenty miles away, where he died.

Mention will be made later of a navvy's wedding at Manton but, in the same week, memories of that joyous event were overshadowed by this accident at Manton tunnel:

> A poor fellow named Wm. Tomlinson, went down about half-way of the shaft in number 2 tunnel to adjust a fire-basket, when by some means the skep in which he stood turned up, and he was precipitated to the bottom, about 40 feet, on his head. His brains protruded through his nose when he was brought to the top of the shaft and his body presented a frightful spectacle: it was conveyed to the Horse and Jockey for the coroner's inquest on Saturday and in the evening of that day his remains were interred in a very respectful manner: he was borne to the grave by six miners. The pall was borne by six banksmen. The subcontractor (Mr. Bugg), the police sergeant and the timekeeper in deep mourning walked first in the procession which was made up by miners and tunnelmen. Men evinced by their serious deportment that they had indeed 'hearts that could feel for another'. (SM 20 August 1847)

Railway employees, too, met with accidents once the line was open and one such accident occurred at Kirby between Syston and Melton:

> On Thursday afternoon the 17th inst. Mr. Thorpe, the station master at Kirby, on the new line of railway between Syston and Melton, met with an accident which was near proving fatal. He was crossing the line just as the train was passing and before he could get across the iron guard of the engine caught him by the dress and threw him down between the rails, the engine and the whole of the train passing over him. On the train stopping and the engineman going to his assistance he was found just within the rails, his head touching one side and his feet the other, so that none of the wheels had gone over him otherwise he must have been killed. As it was, the only injuries he received were some severe contusions on the head and face when thrown down by the engine. Another fortunate circumstance in the case was that the firebox of the engine was placed sufficiently high to admit of its passing over the body without touching it: had it been one of the low boxes Mr. Thorpe must inevitably been crushed to death.
> (SM 25 September 1846)

The first accident to occur between Stamford and Peterborough, in June 1847, involved the wife of the gatekeeper at Uffington station. Observing a favourite dog on the line as a train approached, she attempted to scare the dog away, when her dress was caught by the wheel of the engine. She was thrown against the engine before striking the ground, causing serious spinal injuries. The dog was cut in two.

Falling asleep on duty resulted in the death of a pointsman at Luffenham. Having moved the points, as he was required to do, he then fell asleep until wakened by a passing train, whereupon he rolled over onto the rail and was cut completely in two.

Jumping from moving trains has remained a cause of accidents until the introduction of driver-operated doors. A musician of Manton, riding towards Stamford on a 'luggage' train, jumped from a 'carriage' near South Luffenham and was killed instantly.

If jumping off trains was foolhardy, so was attempting to board moving trains. This caused the death of a carpenter at Manton station when, slipping, he fell between the rails and was sliced in two. He left a widow and two small children.

Idiots, today described as vandals, have been trying to derail trains since the earliest days of railways. Within a month of the line opening between Stamford and Peterborough large stones were placed on the rails near Walton just before the passing of a train. No accident occurred but the Eastern Counties directors offered a £20 reward for the discovery of the offender.

Whether the next man was a vandal, made a human error, or was in need of psychiatric treatment is not clear:

> On Monday last a man who gave his name as Wm. Quid, from the county Galway, Ireland, was brought to Stamford in custody on suspicion of having on that day moved the points on the Syston railway works near the village of North Luffenham whereby one engine was driven into a ballast train, damage done to a large amount and two men seriously hurt. The fellow, after committing the depredation, ran away and was found secreted in Luffenham churchyard. He was conveyed before the magistrates of the county of Rutland for examination.   (SM 4 February 1848)

One would really have expected a more responsible attitude to railway safety from a stationmaster but T. Liddell, holding that position at Stamford in 1853, was fined £5 for 'an offence against the Railway Act'. It appears that he went on a visit to Barrowden and intended to return by the late train from Luffenham to Stamford. Finding that the train had already departed, he began walking along the track until he reached Ketton. Here, 'feeling very tired', he persuaded a porter to move a truck from a siding to the main line, it being Liddell's intention to proceed by gravity to Stamford! The truck, partly laden with beans, came to a stand some distance from Easton level-crossing. Unable to move the wagon himself, he sought the assistance of the gatekeeper and his wife after which he duly arrived at Stamford. This escapade reached the ears of the Midland directors at Derby and he was dismissed from his duties as stationmaster.

It should be appreciated that signalling and the regulation of trains was still rather primitive, even twenty-three years after the opening of the Liverpool & Manchester Railway in 1830. Trains followed one another through a section on the 'time interval' method. After the passing of a stated time, one train was permitted to follow another without knowledge as to the whereabouts of the first train.

It was this method of operating which resulted in an accident to a train from Stamford in 1853. The 8am passenger train from Stamford was approaching Manton station at its usual speed but fog obscured the signals. Wet and slippery rails reduced the effectiveness of the limited braking power available and the passenger train collided with the rear of a stationary goods train. The coupling between the passenger coaches and the engine broke so that the coaches ran backwards down a slight incline. A Stamford dancing teacher, Mrs. Penn, lost several teeth and received many cuts, whilst other passengers were bruised.

THE NAVVIES - II

A typical group of railway navvies. Performing prodigious feats of earth removal, they were not always treated fairly by the contractors who employed them.

(Arthur Jordan

Railway navvies generally received a bad press throughout the years of railway construction but, as the following case shows, their actions were not always without justification.

Fielding Moore, a subcontractor on the Syston-Peterborough line, made it a condition of payment to his men that they should drink a quart of ale at the Anchor public house where he paid the wages, or submit to the price of a quart being deducted from the wages due. On one particular night 780 navvies were brought into Stamford from distances of up to twelve miles to receive their wages. There were disputes over amounts due which lasted until gone 10pm, after which it was too late for the men to make their way back to their homes or lodgings in Luffenham, Morcott, Manton and other villages. Not surprisingly, large groups of navvies wandered the streets causing 'serious apprehensions as to the peace and safety of the town'. (SM 4 February 1848)

Withholding payment of wages due to navvies was a recurring cause of hardship to the men and their families as well as disturbances for which the men, rather than their employers, have usually been blamed:

The town of Stamford has been in some peril this week from the misconduct of persons connected with the works on the railway, in a grade which might be expected to exempt society from terror on their account. Owing to a disagreement between Mr. Worswick, the contractor for executing a great portion of the railway from Syston to Peterboro', and Mr. Chester, his sub-contractor, the labourers on the line eastward from Stamford were not paid their wages on Saturday evening past; and as some delay in this respect had been experienced on a former occasion, the men on Monday became clamorous, refused to continue their work and assembled in great numbers at Stamford... The dispute coming to the knowledge of the men, they became vociferous in the streets, and Mr. Roberts was in danger of being very roughly handled by them. On his going over the bridge he was followed by a party whose movements indicated an intention of throwing him over the parapet and into the river: he however succeeded in getting clear of them and hastily made to the George Inn to which he was followed by the 'navvies' and was loudly threatened by them. In order to save him from being pulled to pieces the servants in the booking office in the Inn yard thrust him into an inner room, the door of which the assailants speedily broke open; but fortunately it was practicable to get him upstairs before they entered; and after he had run through a whole suite of rooms, and fastened the door of each as he quitted, he was at last concealed in a cock-loft known only to a few of the servants, and was thus lost to his pursuers. After a considerable time he was supplied with a dress as a disguise, and was got out of the inn in a fly and driven to Ketton. During all this time the navvies were on the watch, and it was feared that some outrage would be committed in the town in the course of the night, as many of the men declared that they had had nothing to eat for two days ... To each of 300 or 400 men sums were due, the want of which really prevented their obtaining any food for themselves or their families, as the tradespeople of Stamford and the villages refused to give them credit ... Mr. Chester, it was added, could supply the men with beer which he himself sold to them, and which he set off against their wages when the instalments took place, but he would supply them with nothing else and now they could not obtain any money from him to purchase bread or other necessaries ...

(SM 19 June 1846)

Five months later another case of a contractor refusing to pay men for work done came before the magistrates when they 'expressed their unqualified opinion that the applicants were entitled to what they demanded'.

In another instance at Luffenham a man absconded with the wages for men he had employed to work on the contract. The editor of the Stamford Mercury complained of the 'abominable tyranny' of contractors who would only pay at fortnightly intervals and on a fixed day. Consequently, men moving from one contract to another, for whatever reason, frequently had to return over considerable distances to obtain the wages they had earned. This prompted a letter from a contractor's manager expressing the view that 'a spirit of independence now prevails among the working class which, for the want of principle and judgement, leads many into excesses which it would be impossible for the employer to submit to'.

Cases concerning men not being paid for the work performed continued to come before the Stamford magistrates. In March 1848 thirty men complained that a sub-contractor refused to pay them any part of what was due to them for the proceeding fortnight's work, and that they were without the means of subsistence. The magistrates feared possible unrest if such cases persisted. A week later, another case was before the magistrates when sixteen labourers working on the St. Martin's tunnel were without support because the sub-contractor had absconded with the wages due to them. Shortly after this fifty-nine navvies complained to the magistrates that they had been dismissed without notice and had been unable to obtain wages due for their previous week's work. Some of them, and their families, were starving. No settlement appearing likely, the offending Mr. Berney:

> . . .found himself beset at his lodgings in St. Martin's by a large number of the men who threatened violence to him unless he paid the wages which were their due; and he requested of the Mayor to be allowed to take refuge in the Town Hall. This of course was granted ... The above was the fifth time within eighteen months that the magistrates of Stamford had been called upon to intercede between contractors and workmen ...   (SM 9 June 1848)

Navvies at Manton tunnel were indicted for rioting in July 1847. It was alleged that a gang of more than a hundred English navvies, working at the north end of the tunnel, had armed themselves with bludgeons with which to attack about twelve Irish navvies working at the south end. The Irish were driven away but returned later when they were again attacked. Following this the Irish again escaped and they had not been seen since. Two of the English navvies were found guilty of riot and sentenced to two months imprisonment.

Several times the navvies appeared before the magistrates on lesser charges. In February 1846 two men were convicted of trespass in pursuit of game at Barnack and sentenced to hard labour in the House of Correction for a month, unless the penalty of twenty shillings each be paid sooner.

Working on the Sabbath, except in certain occupations, remained an offence until almost the end of the century. Five navvies were charged with working on the line at Kirby Bellars and fined five shillings each. A youthful driver of a horse and cart engaged upon the railway works was fined sixteen shillings, which included costs, for not having 'command and government of the animal'. The horse, with the cart, had charged through the streets 'with great violence'.

A navvy was charged with stealing nine pieces of deal, value nine pence which he used as firewood in his hut. A fortnight's imprisonment with hard labour was his punishment. Transportation for nine years was the penalty paid by two navvies who stole meat at Gunthorpe, but a railway contractor, who resisted a police constable while in the execution of his duty, got off with a fine of thirty shillings.

If a letter to the local press is to be believed then life in navvy camps was 'la dolce vita'

> A stranger visiting the works at the tunnel here [Manton] would conjecture it to be a modern colony for free trade as beer, spirits, game, and all commodities usually requiring licences in other parts of the country are openly sold by the occupiers of the huts built for the convenience of excavators employed upon the line: in addition, these gentlemen of the navvy gangs who have a taste for field sports explore the

neighbouring preserves in great numbers on Sundays and holiday occasions, without any terror of gamekeepers or those 'potent, grave and reverend seigniors, whose edict from the rural star chamber rarely fails to consign the luckless peasant (should curiosity induce him to probe his stick in a rabbit hole) to the society of felons. This enlightened extension of the free trade scheme has greatly reduced the price of game: pheasants, which hitherto have rarely gone elsewhere than among the select grades of society, now find their way to nearly all tables. (SM 6 November 1846)

There was undoubtedly a considerable amount of hyperbole in this account but, if even half were true, can these men be blamed? Performing prodigious feats of construction surpassing those of the Egyptians in building the Pyramids, the navvies, as we have seen, were frequently cheated out of their earnings or stood off without notice, whilst they and their families received no compensation for their frequent serious injuries.

Generally there was strong camaraderie among these men, extending to financial support for fellow navvies and their families meeting with misfortune. Joyous occasions were also shared as the following shows:

On Monday se'nnight this village [Manton] was a scene of mirth and holiday; one of the miners took a young woman "for better, for worse". The works seemed at a dead stand - no sound echoed from the tunnel beneath, and the hoarse note of the banksman was not heard on the shafts above with his 'back up, back up'. About 10 o'clock great numbers had congregated in the churchyard, and in a few minutes a band of music played a favourite air. The wedding party was soon at the church, where the workmen had filed in triple lines to admit the smiling group: the utmost decorum prevailed and one spirit pervaded the whole. The knot being tied, the bride, bridegroom, etc passed in the same order while a few laughable jokes were passed. The band struck up again and the bells pealed out. The merrymaking now began and the day was spent in glee: the rustic dance was kept up beneath the wide canopy of heaven till the evening closed. (SM 20 August 1847)

OTHER RAILWAYS TO STAMFORD

Whilst controversy raged as to whether the Syston & Peterborough line should go north or south of the Welland there was considerable agitation to persuade the Great Northern Railway to route its main line from London to York through Stamford. The Stamford Mercury blamed the Marquess of Exeter entirely for Stamford being avoided but there is evidence suggesting that other factors influenced the Great Northern to pass through Peterborough rather than Stamford.

It has already been explained that, prior to 1850, the rail route from London to York was over the London & North Western to Rugby, then the Midland to Normanton, and finally the York & North Midland. 'King Hudson' (his derogatory nickname) controlled both the Midland and Y&NM so that any proposal for a direct line from London to York was seen by him as a threat to his so-called empire.

'Railway Mania' and railway rivalry resulted in several proposals for a more direct line between London and York. Originally 'Great Northern' was the title of a railway proposed but rejected by the House of Commons in 1836. Its route would have been from Whitechapel, London via Cambridge, Sleaford, Lincoln and Doncaster.

RAILWAYS AROUND STAMFORD 1845 - 1867

A Direct Northern Railway was surveyed by Sir John Rennie and William Gravatt along a route through Peterborough, Lincoln, Gainsborough and Selby. Another proposal was for a Cambridge & York Railway, surveyed by James Walker who had earlier drawn-up similar plans in 1835. This line would have connected with the Eastern Counties for entry to London, but later Walker was asked to survey for a line all the way through to London.

Next the Eastern Counties, with Robert Stephenson as its engineer, proposed extensions of the Cambridge & York line to include Lincoln, Gainsborough and Doncaster. Finally, a Great Northern Railway was surveyed by Joseph Gibbs from London via Huntingdon, Stamford, Grantham, Newark, Gainsborough and Doncaster, this being the first mention of a line passing through Stamford.

In 1844 the Cambridge & York changed its title to the London & York, taking a route via Cambridge, Peterborough, Spalding, Sleaford and Lincoln. Edmund Denison, later to become Chairman of the Great Northern Railway, at a meeting in Peterborough in August 1844 presided over by Earl Fitzwilliam, stated that he would never consent to sacrifice the wider interests of the general public for the benefit of any town on the route. 'Our main object is to shorten the distance between London and Yorkshire. If a line through Peterborough is best for the general public, Peterborough shall have it, but, if not, it shall pass outside the town' he declared. A few days later Joseph Locke presented his report which was adopted and which proposed a route through Peterborough and east of Stamford. That surely ruled out Stamford being on the main line?

By this time George Hudson had taken over the chairmanship of the Eastern Counties Railway thus adding it to his group of companies. Since he could not prevent the making of an alternative route between London and York he now sought to have two of his companies, the Eastern Counties and the York & North Midland, as part of such a route. In 1845 the Eastern Counties submitted a scheme for an extension from Cambridge through Lincoln and Doncaster to South Milford, there to join the York & North Midland into York.

Since the Great Northern and the London & York had similar objectives, a joint committee was formed and adopted the title London & York. William Cubitt became the engineer after Joseph Locke resigned. Plans were deposited for the 1845 session of Parliament for the largest railway project so far, consisting of:

A.   The main line to York.

B.   A loop line from Peterborough to Bawtry via Boston.

C.   A branch from Bawtry to Sheffield.

D.   A branch from Doncaster to Wakefield.

There were to be branches to various towns including Stamford.

A committee of the Board of Trade, which had the responsibility for railways, was set-up to sift through the 224 Railway Bills before Parliament and to recommend acceptance or rejection. Whilst the L&Y Bill passed both the Standing Orders

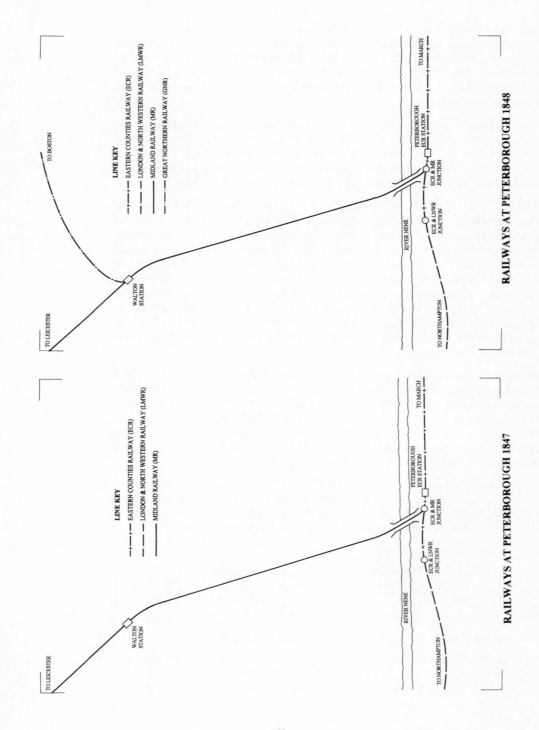

RAILWAYS AT PETERBOROUGH 1848

RAILWAYS AT PETERBOROUGH 1847

Committee and a Second Reading in the House of Commons, it was too late for the present session of the Lords. It now become known that the Board of Trade committee was recommending rejection of the L&Y scheme.

A surprising twist saw the Direct Northern decide to amalgamate with the London & York, following which the title 'Great Northern' was adopted from 30 May 1846. In the meantime the L&Y Bill (which did not include Stamford on its main line) received Royal Assent on 26 June 1846. Other lines proposed but not proceeded with were the Stamford & Spalding Railway, and a Boston, Stamford & Birmingham Railway. According to the Stamford Mercury (15 January 1847) the Great Northern had applied to purchase property belonging to the Stamford Corporation on the east side of the town. The intended line was to cross the Uffington road 'near the milestone at Beggar's Nook' and a large station was to be erected 'near the site of the Boiling House on the Ryhall road at the back of the Infirmary'.

During 1847 various Bills for deviations from the Great Northern line, as approved by the Act of the previous year, were considered by Parliament. One of these sought to divert the main line through Stamford:

> The affairs of the Great Northern Railway and their probable influence on the prosperity and the peace of Stamford are at this time the sole subject of conversation here. To ascertain who has been to blame for sending away the line to a distance of 4 or 5 miles from the town, when the deviation Bill which is at present before Parliament was designed for bringing it within the borough - and to take measures for obviating if possible so injurious a result of the adverse report of the Committee of the House of Commons - has been the business of the Stamford committee appointed at the Town Hall on Tuesday se'nnight. A deputation was sent to London on Friday last and a second deputation on Monday, with the view of interceding first with the Marquess of Exeter, and next with the board of directors of the railway, for a restoration of good understanding between the parties, so that the interests of the town might not be sacrificed by their disagreement as to the terms on which the noble Marquess should be remunerated for the 40 acres of his land (lying between Barnack and Ryhall) which will be required for the railway line and for the station which it was intended to build near Newstead tollbar. With the deepest concern we announce that all the efforts of the deputations, aided as they were by the unceasing solicitions of Sir John Trollope (who on both occasions accompanied the deputations to London) have been unsuccessful. The Marquess of Exeter demands such a price for his land as the railway directors declare they have not been required to pay in any other part of the line, and as their duty to those for whose interests they act compel them to decline. Whilst the members of the second deputation were sitting in the Railway Board room on Tuesday evening the ultimatum of the directors was despatched by an express messenger to Lord Exeter at Ascot races, and the messenger returned to town on Wednesday with His Lordship's rejection of the terms. The proposition was that the company should pay the Marquess 80 years' purchase of the rental of the land, and such rental to be established on the valuation of competent judges to be approved by His Lordship without reference to the comparatively low rental at which (for whatever purpose) it may be at present let. Lord Exeter has

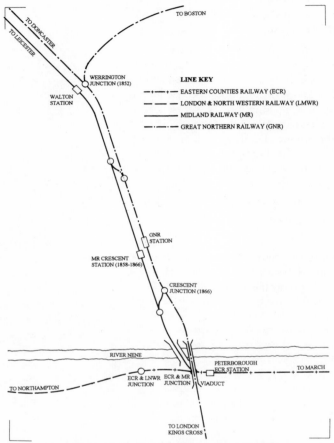

LINE KEY

———→——— EASTERN COUNTIES RAILWAY (ECR)
— — — — LONDON & NORTH WESTERN RAILWAY (LMWR)
——————— MIDLAND RAILWAY (MR)
—·—·—·— GREAT NORTHERN RAILWAY (GNR)

RAILWAYS AT PETERBOROUGH 1850/1866

refused to abide by the valuation of any other person whatever, and will treat only upon his own basis (understood to be £600 an acre for the land) which he declares to be not excessive for the great residenciary inconvenience and other consequences to which the bringing of the railway to Stamford must lead. The affair therefore seems now to be without hope. The Parliamentary committee, it is true, have not yet made their report to the House, but they are expected to do so this evening (Friday); and if no member should move for the recommitment of the Bill, and succeed in his motion, the Great Northern Railway is lost to the town of Stamford.

(SM 4 June 1847)

When the Great Northern opened its Loop line through Boston, Sleaford and Lincoln to Doncaster in October 1848, a junction was made with the Syston & Peterborough line at Walton, 2 1/2 miles north of the present Peterborough station. Walton was a station on the Midland but not on the GN. Great Northern trains then ran over Midland metals to terminate at the Eastern Counties station in Peterborough, which now had the distinction of accommodating the trains of four separate railway companies; EC, LNW, MR and GN.

Completion of the line from King's Cross to Walton Junction in August 1850 saw the Great Northern open its own Peterborough station, known as Priestgate. The junction with the Midland at Walton was now taken out and GN trains off the Loop line terminated at the new Peterborough station. This made it difficult for passengers from the Stamford line to connect with Great Northern trains, since interchange between the Eastern Counties station and the Great Northern station involved crossing Peterborough's streets.

Opening of the Great Northern's Towns line through Grantham to Doncaster (it never reached York over its own metals) on 1 August 1852 required a junction with the Loop line at Walton, now known as Werrington Junction.

From 1858 the Midland opened its own Peterborough station named 'Crescent', almost opposite the Great Northern station, and trains called there before terminating at the Eastern Counties station.

Crescent station was closed in 1866 when two junctions enabled Midland trains to call at the Great Northern station before going on to the Eastern Counties (Great Eastern from 1862) station. Stamford passengers could now make connections at the Great Northern station without difficulty.

With the Great Northern main line well under construction some 4 miles to the east of Stamford attention was turned to securing a branch from Tallington. The Mercury's vendetta against the Marquess of Exeter was relentless:

> ... should the directors [of the GNR] in the course of the next two or three years introduce to Parliament a Bill for a branch line and be well supported by the inhabitants of Stamford, the Marquess of Exeter's opposition will be boldly defied and the case put to the House of Commons on its real merits independent of private interests. We are told that if the company could have established here a grand mid-way station... the benefits which would have accrued to tradesmen and the owners of house property would have been sensibly felt before the present time but the interposition of Lord Exeter, the neighbour and patron, of the borough, has effectually dispelled all hope of improvement for some time to come.
>
> (SM 14 June 1850)

Tapping the South Yorkshire coalfield, the Great Northern promised supplies competitive with those of Midlands pits. Messrs. Handson and Knight, Stamford coal merchants, secured the leasehold of the Stamford Navigation in 1850 with a view to a connecting wharf with the Great Northern at Tallington. 'It is contemplated that it [the Navigation] may be made the route of a branch railway to connect Stamford and Tallington and thus give full advantage to the railway works which are about to be opened'. (SM 2 August 1850)

Whilst the Towns line was still under construction Stamford was petitioning that Tallington be made the station for Bourne, Stamford, Uffington and Deeping but Bourne people were asking that Essendine be the main station. Although Essendine

Looking west from Peterborough East station the London & North Western lines run straight ahead; the Midland lines branch off to the right; whilst the Great Northern main line is carried across on the viaduct.

(Arthur Jordan collection)

was made a 'First Class Station', i.e. one at which First Class trains called, this did not prevent the Earl of Lindsey securing a judgement requiring the Great Northern to stop express trains at Tallington whenever a First Class ticket holder presented himself/herself at that station.

Until Stamford was connected by rail to Essendine in 1856 passengers made their way between Stamford and Tallington station by horse-drawn omnibus, unless they possessed their own equipages.

During the years of controversy over the Great Northern's route to York the London & North Western had been approaching Stamford from the west. Often referred to as the Rugby & Stamford Railway, work had commenced as early as 1846. Mainly for financial reasons, work was delayed several times before the section between Rugby and Market Harborough was opened on 29th April 1850, with three trains per day each way.

By June 1st the line had reached Caldecott, where the station was named Rockingham, no doubt in deference to the nearby castle seat of the Watsons. The castle was an early venue for an excursion:

RAILWAY TRIP FROM MARKET HARBOROUGH TO ROCKINGHAM CASTLE. The Honorable Richard Watson having kindly responded to an application for permission to visit the Castle and grounds belonging thereto, a committee was appointed on Monday evening 29th ult. for the arrangement of a party, and handbills were distributed the next morning purporting that all persons intending to avail themselves of a visit to the ancient domains of Rockingham were to obtain tickets of the parties comprising the committee for a trip to Rockingham on

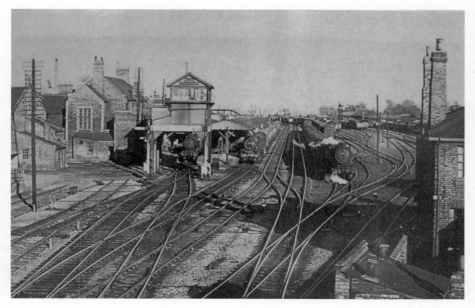

This view of Peterborough East station shows the London & North Western and Midland Railway lines from the bottom left with the Eastern Counties line to March disappearing in the centre and on the right the extensive sidings used by all three companies.

(Arthur Jordan collection)

Friday 2nd inst. It was calculated that there might be between two and three hundred applicants, but 300 tickets were soon disposed of, and from Harborough and the neighbourhood the number considerably exceeded the calculation. Seventeen carriages were completely filled, and many more were ready at Medbourne bridge, and the carriages were at length in a clustered state. From the station to the park, a distance of more than a mile, there was a complete file of visitants, proceeded by a band of music. Such a concourse of people the inhabitants of Rockingham had never seen before, the schoolboys welcoming them, as they walked up, with their flags and huzzas. The four o'clock pm train from Harborough conveyed several hundred more, and so unexpected was the number at this hour, that they were obliged to bring into requisition the cattle carriages, inappropriate as they were for holiday clothes. It may be said that, from all quarters there were not less than three thousand persons. All appeared truly delighted, and expressed their highest admiration of the extensive views, flower gardens, and shrubberies, and the various grottoes and groves. There was also a variety of sports for young and old, cricketing, quoits, dancing (in several parties), swinging round a pole and leaping over a cord at the time, etc; the band playing at intervals and keeping up the hilarity till the hour of retiring. Unfortunately, the spirits of many were severely dampened by having to wait for the carriages to convey them home. So unexpected was the number that the Stationmaster at Harborough had to send to Rugby twice for more carriages and another engine, which caused a delay at Rockingham station of more than two hours, at which place there was no accommodation for refreshment, excepting the pump, of which many availed themselves. At length they arrived at Harborough station at ten minutes past eleven o'clock, in 35 carriages pulled by two engines. There were more than two thousand first and second-class tickets issued at Harborough station that day. We have the satisfaction of adding as much to the credit of all parties, that the servants at the Castle went over the grounds the following morning, and declared that no injury whatever had been done.   (NM 10 August 1850)

By a junction at Luffenham (25½ miles from Rugby) the LNW exercised running powers over the Midland to Stamford. There was to have been a LNW terminus station a short distance west of Nun's Farm at Stamford but when the service commenced on 2 June1851 trains ran into the Midland station. This 'temporary' arrangement was to remain in force until the Rugby-Stamford line closed in 1966. A LNW engine shed at Stamford existed from 1881 until 1926. At opening three trains ran daily in each direction between Rugby and Stamford.

An unusual event involving a pedestrian and a steam engine was staged on this line:

A NOVEL RACE - A few days ago, a singular race came off between a pedestrian and a steam engine. A Scotchman who resides at Market Harborough, wagered a sovereign with a person of Medbourn, to run from Medbourn station on the Rugby and Stamford Railway to the Town Hall steps at Harborough. The former to have 15 minutes advance of the other and to take what directions he might choose, the latter to go by train to Harborough station and then to run from thence to the place appointed. Everything was well arranged by both parties and the match was won by the Scotchman beating his opponent with two minutes to spare
                                                                    .(NM 30 November 1850)

This view of Stamford station shows the island platform with the Seaton train bay on the right.

(Elisabeth Jordan)

Reference has been made to the Great Northern making Essendine a 'First Class' station rather than Tallington, against the wishes of Stamford people. An Act for the Stamford & Essendine Railway was passed in August 1853 and for this the Marquess of Exeter was prominent in its promotion. It is said that the Marquess came to repent his alleged opposition to the Great Northern passing through Stamford and so promoted the S&E. Be that as it may, it was anticipated that a connection with the GN would bring Yorkshire coals into Stamford at 2 shillings less per ton than those conveyed by the Midland from Leicestershire collieries.

At Essendine this railway's junction with the Great Northern was such that trains arriving from Stamford faced northwards rather than towards London. In the 3½ miles of single line to Stamford there was just one station, Ryhall & Belmesthorpe. At Stamford a station was erected at the end of Water Street, on the site of the earlier Midland temporary station. A junction between the Stamford & Essendine and the Midland line for the exchange of goods traffic was installed.

Perhaps the occupant of Burghley House's connection with this railway influenced the choice of an Elizabethan style for the station which prominently displayed the Exeter coat of arms. Architect William Hurst arranged for the main door to open into a spacious booking-hall above which a gallery, with a wrought-iron balustrade, gave access to the Company's boardroom and offices. A lantern roof provided adequate daylight in the booking-hall.

An island platform stood within a covered train shed which, for some forty years, engines did not enter. Arriving trains were halted at the station throat and the engines detached, leaving the coaches to run forward by gravity. In addition to a goods shed, an engine shed and turntable were provided. Without ceremony services began on 1 November 1856.

Although the Stamford & Essendine was an independent company its services were operated by the Great Northern for 50% of the gross revenue. In 1859 the line was doubled but to no avail, passengers preferred the Midland to Peterborough and then Great Northern, thus avoiding long waits at Essendine for connections. The agreement with the GN expired in 1892 after which the line was taken over on permanent lease by that company.

The S&E station was known as 'Stamford Water Street' until changed in 1950 to 'East'. Closed to passenger traffic in 1957 (goods 1963) Essendine trains ran into the ex-Midland station, known as 'Stamford Town', until 1959.

Although not opened until eleven years after the Stamford & Essendine, a Stamford & Wansford Railway had been under consideration from as early as 1847. The London & North Western Railway obtained an Act in 1847 for a line from Bletchley through Newport Pagnell, Olney and Wellingborough to Wansford and Stamford. '... thus the town of Stamford will secure nearly a direct line to London by the Birmingham Railway'.(SM 26 February 1847)

In May of that year it was confidently anticipated that the Wansford-Stamford section would be completed by the coming November. In 1846, at the same time as the Saxby deviation, the Midland had obtained authorisation for a Stamford-Wansford line. However, by July 1848, no progress being made, members of the Stamford Town Council were in London hoping to meet George Hudson of the Midland on the matter. Hudson being away, Mr. Herries, MP for Stamford, who was likely to be at Burghley, promised that he and his colleague would discuss the matter with the Marquess of Exeter '... who had not opposed the projected railway from Stamford to Wansford and was understood to have no objection to it' (SM 7 July 1848)

Two weeks later the Mayor reported that a deputation on railway business had met the Marquess of Exeter who had promised his support and would write to Hudson on the matter. It was believed that Hudson would agree to surrender to the LNW the right to construct the Wansford-Stamford line.

A worsening financial situation explains why neither the Midland nor the London & North Western made this desired rail link. As George Hudson put it: 'Without money what the d ... l can we do? We have not the means of executing more important works than this.' (SM 4 August 1848)

Sixteen years later the Stamford & Essendine Company obtained an Act to construct a 6¼ mile, single line link from its Stamford station to a junction with the London & North Western at Sibson on the east side of the River Nene. Running powers enabled its trains to enter the LNW Wansford station. Intermediate stations were at Barnack, Ufford Bridge and Wansford Road. The route followed was that authorised in the Midland Railway Act of 1846.

A difference between the Marquess and the LNW resulted in the junction being severed, so that from 1 Jan 1870 trains terminated at a wooden platform known as Sibson. From January 1872 the Great Northern took over the line, following which the junction was restored from May 1873.

As with the Stamford-Essendine line, the Stamford-Wansford line offered no improvement for Stamford-London passengers who continued to use the Midland to Peterborough and then GN to King's Cross. In July 1929 the line was closed to both passenger and goods traffic.

Stamford's East station carried on accommodating the Essendine traffic until 1957, when passenger trains were diverted to the ex-Midland Town station. The Stamford-Essendine line continued to carry both passenger and goods traffic until June 1959. Goods traffic was handled at East until 1963.

If the Great Northern main line had passed through Stamford rather than Peterborough, what difference would that have made to the town's prosperity, to the quality of life in this town with the greatest number of listed buildings in the land? Would Stamford have been the location for the filming of 'Middlemarch'?

At the time of the decision for the Great Northern to avoid Stamford an official of that company painted a picture of what might have been:

> An agent who was in the town a few days ago estimated that nearly 1,000 souls (including the families of clerks, porters, artisans and others) would have been added to the population of Stamford and as much as £50,000 a year would have been spent in the place by the company and their servants if the depot had been constructed here as proposed (SM 27 September 1850)

The above estimated population increase fell far short of what happened at Peterborough. In 1851 Stamford's population was 9,000 and Peterborough only 8,763 but twenty years later the figures were 8,193 and 17,429. In 1901 Peterborough's population had risen to 30,872 whilst Stamford's remained stagnant at 8,229.

Disappointed or pleased that Stamford did not become a railway town, its present-day residents should at least be thankful that Stamford is still served by trains, which is more than can be claimed by several much larger towns.

APPENDIX
PROPERTY OWNERS and OCCUPIERS IN 1844

No.	Description	Owner	Lessee	Occupier
PARISH OF ST JOHN				
15	Pathway between Lammas & George bridges	Marquess of Exeter		
PARISH OF ST MARY				
12	Shop, yard, garden, houses, & premises	Marquess of Exeter		Jane North Richard Whitehead George William
Bunning				
23	Part of Bridge	Marquess of Exeter	Robert Hunt	
25	Warehouses	Horatio Thos Gilchrist or Marquess of Exeter	John Congreve	John Congreve Charles Lowe Richard Wade Oliver Wade
35	Timber yard & saw pit	Marquess of Exeter		Thomas Smith
27	Wharf	Mayor, Aldermen & Burgesses of Stamford	Sir Felix Buckley & William Harper	
22	Street	Commissioners for Improvement of Stamford		
PARISH OF ST GEORGE				
3	Waggon shed	Robert Hunt		In hand
4	Timber yard & sheds	Robert Hunt		William Hind
5	Boathouse, shed & yard	William Harper		In hand
6	Tan yard, buildings & grass	Marquess of Exeter		William Bowker
12	Warehouse, shed, wharf & yard	Thomas Handson		In hand
16	Occupation road	Thos Handson & Stamford St Martin's Gas Company		
14	Gasworks, gasometer, buildings garden, yard & premises	Stamford & St Martin's Gas Company		In hand
17	Warehouse, buildings, yard & wharf	Stamford & St Martin's Gas Company		Joseph Cook Grant
18	Workshops & Stone yard	Stamford & St Martin's Gas Company		Robert Woolstone
38	Cottage & garden	George Luff		In hand

39	Street	Commissioners for Improvement of Stamford	
37	Garden, grass & outbuilding	William Thos Nuezam	In hand
46	Summer house & garden	James Althorpe	In hand
47	Building, yard & garden	Thos Hippersley Jackson	In hand
48	Garden	Earl Brownlow	John Strether
49	Grass	Earl Brownlow	In hand
50	Occupation rd & wharf	Earl Brownlow	
19	Cottage & vacant land	Stamford & St Martin's Gas Company	George Jones
20	6 Cottages, gardens & outbuildings	William Hind	John Close Charles Walker James Sissmore Thos Henderson William Andrews John Sherrett
32	Street	Commissioners for Improvement of Stamford	
33	Coach house	Thos Wilkington	In hand
34	5 Cottages, yards & garden	William Hickling	William Littledyke William Jordan Edward Gray Empty Elizabeth Hibbins
35	Garden	Earl Brownlow	John Strether
36	8 Cottages & yards	Goodliffe Jeffs	Edward Pope William Dursley Julia Keen John Sharpe Empty Samuel Ellis Empty Gilbert Wilson
40	Street	Commissioners for Improvement of Stamford	
41	Street	Commissioners for Improvement of Stamford	
44	2 Cottages	William Rear Horden	Thomas Ward William Alderman
45	Garden	Earl Brownlow	John Strether
50	Occupation rd & wharf	Earl Brownlow	

51	Cottage & garden	Earl Brownlow	John Strether William Chambers John Roberts Joseph Cook Grant Robert Littledyke George Dolby Thomas Woodward Henry Gilbert
52	Grass	Earl Brownlow	William Strether
52a	Pond	Earl Brownlow	
56a	Grass	Marquess of Exeter	James Pollard
56	Grass, building & pond	Marquess of Exeter	William Nutt
57	Grass & building	Marquess of Exeter	Francis Simpson
58	Grass	Marquess of Exeter	John Palmer
59	Grass & stable	Marquess of Exeter	James Simpson
60	Grass	Marquess of Exeter	Joshua Lumby
61	Grass	Marquess of Exeter	Joshua Lumby
62	Grass	Marquess of Exeter	William Bowker
63	Grass	Marquess of Exeter	William Fenton
64	Grass	Marquess of Exeter	William Fenton
75	Grass & footpath	Mayor, Aldermen & Burgesses of Stamford & Surveyors of Highways	Robert Palmer
76	Canal, locks & bridge	Mayor, Aldermen & Burgesses of Stamford	Sir Felix Buckley William Harper
77	Garden, osier bed & pond	ditto	Robert Palmer Rebecca Whitham
81	Plantation	ditto	Robert Palmer Rebecca Whitham
82	Garden	ditto	Robert Palmer Rebecca Whitham
83	Mill buildings, stream & premises	ditto	Robert Palmer
84	Grass & bridle road	ditto & Surveyors of Highways	Robert Palmer Thomas Bentham
85	Grass	Marquess of Exeter	Charles Spencer Benjamin Frisby
86	Grass	Marquess of Exeter	John Dalton
91	Grass & footpath	Marquess of Exeter & Surveyors of Highways	Ruth Roberts Thomas Roberts
93	Grass & footpath	ditto	William Scholes

PARISH OF ST MARTINIS

1	Occupation Rd	Marquess of Exeter		
2	Grass	Marquess of Exeter	Guardians of the Poor Isaac Lumby for the Parish of St Martin's	
3	Part of the river	Marquess of Exeter		
4	Grass, footpath & stack yard	Marquess of Exeter & Surveyors of Highways		Frederick Lumby
5	Arable & hovel	Rev Plumpton Wilson		George Denny
6	Grass & outbuilding	ditto		George Denny
7	Grass & building	ditto		William Bowker Thomas Bainton
8	Arable	ditto		Richard Prous
9	Arable & footpath	Marquess of Exeter & Surveyors of Highways		Thomas Woodroof
10	Grass & pond	Marquess of Exeter		George Coles
11	Occupation rd	Marquess of Exeter		
12	Grass	Marquess of Exeter	Thomas Baxter	
13	Grass & Footpath	Marquess of Exeter & Surveyors of Highways		John Pollard
14	Grass & footpath	ditto		Robert Middleton
15	Bridle road	Surveyors of Highways		
16	Grass	Marquess of Exeter		John Smith
17	Grass & footpath	Marquess of Exeter & Surveyors of Highways		William Thornay Nuezam
19	Grass & footpath	ditto		Timothy Lincoln
20	Arable	Marquess of Exeter		John Pollard
21	Occupation rd	Marquess of Exeter		
22	Grass, footpath & pond	Marquess of Exeter & Surveyors of Highways		John Dalton
23	Arable	Marquess of Exeter		John Smith
24	Grass	Marquess of Exeter		Jeremiah Pollard